DON'T APPLAUD.
EITHER LAUGH OR DON'T.
(AT THE COMEDY CELLAR)

ANDREW HANKINSON

DON'T APPLAUD. EITHER LAUGH OR DON'T.

At the Comedy Cellar

SCRIBE

Melbourne • London

Scribe Publications
2 John St, Clerkenwell, London, WC1N 2ES, United Kingdom
18–20 Edward St, Brunswick, Victoria 3056, Australia
3754 Pleasant Ave, Suite 100, Minneapolis, Minnesota 55409, USA

First published by Scribe 2020
This edition published 2021

Typeset in Adobe Garamond by the publishers

Printed and bound in the UK by CPI Group (UK) Ltd, Croydon CR0 4YY

Scribe Publications is committed to the sustainable use of natural resources and the use of paper products made responsibly from those resources.

9781950354542 (US edition)
9781911617686 (UK edition)
9781925713541 (Australian edition)
9781925693690 (ebook)

Catalogue records for this book are available from the National Library of Australia and the British Library.

scribepublications.com
scribepublications.co.uk
scribepublications.com.au

For my wife and children

CHAPTER 204

Noam Dworman, owner of the Comedy Cellar, is at home in Ardsley, a small town up the Hudson from Manhattan. There are lots of trees. The author phones him,

Author: So you wouldn't have been surprised?

Noam: The world wouldn't have been. I mean, there was a guy named … Jesus Christ … Poindexter? Was it Poindexter?

Author: With the feminism thing?

Noam: No, it was during the Iran-Contra hearings. One of those guys, I can't remember his name. Bud McFarlane. He had been humiliated and he tried to kill himself, and that example always stayed with me. I know people think I'm the one with no empathy, but when you imagine what it's like to essentially go on the world's sexual offenders list, except every single person knows about it, and your children are carrying your last name, and you've lost everything, and you don't know if you can work again, and you can't walk down the street, and you can't go in a restaurant, everybody's staring at you, is it so surprising to think that somebody might say, "Listen, I'm checking out?"

Author: I think it doesn't cross a lot of people's minds, the people who pile on with these things.

Noam: It doesn't cross a lot of people's minds?

Author: Yeah. I think the people who pile on, who get really angry … Whenever something like that happens I have empathy with basically everyone involved and I try not to make it worse for anyone, but some people who are piling on, I think they're never thinking that Louis is vulnerable or upset, they don't care about him, they're just thinking he needs punishment and, "How can we get him?"

Noam: This is a comment I've usually made when somebody has talked about the fact that, "Oh boo hoo, he hasn't suffered," and I say, "Do you really think he hasn't suffered? Because would you have been surprised if he had strung himself up? If you wouldn't have been surprised if he strung himself up then clearly you recognize there's some suffering going on." That's kind of where I was coming from. It's totally disingenuous. It's like, I hate Saddam Hussein, but when they picked him up in that spider hole, would I say he's not suffering? Yeah, he's suffering. You could say, "Good, I'm glad he's suffering," but what they try to do, and I see this through so many areas now when I think about it, how dehumanization is the first step to bigotry, it's so interesting, it really is, you have to find a way to discount them as human beings, and then it's an open road in front of you. So they can't accept that he's suffering at all, because the whole premise is this is all okay because he hasn't suffered. And it's not honest. Yes, he's suffered enormously. That doesn't mean that he didn't deserve it, but don't pretend he hasn't suffered enormously. Then you have to decide, is it enough?

CHAPTER 203

Author: It's getting nasty though.

Noam: Is it getting nasty? I think it's calming down.

Author: Do you think it's calming down? Well, maybe. I don't know.

Noam: Why's it getting nasty?

Author: I think people will gather themselves … It's all just stuff online. Even that firebomb tweet that you had. People are taking against things, and it's people who are very angry anyway and feel they want to have a fight for some reason, but it's not necessarily people who are thinking things through carefully.

Noam: Listen, I went down there for the first time to watch him, because I hadn't really watched him in person all through this, and I was really struck by how small this was. This tiny room, and ninety-five people watching him, and they're all laughing. And yes, this is a man who did something shameful in his past, not exactly unique to Planet Earth in that way, and when you take away from that this nonsense that's said about us, the way we're treating women, and the way we're a gatekeeper, and, like, "Dworman is such a powerful figure," and all this nonsense, really, you know, then you say this is such a small event. It's a man, a broken man, kind of speaking to a small group of people who are voluntarily listening to him and laughing, yet hundreds of millions of people who couldn't find Yemen on a map regard this as vitally important to the world. It's like, guys, it's stunning.

CHAPTER 202

Noam and the author sit in Noam's office at his home,

Author: I go backwards and forwards in my head, trying to figure it out, because I was in the room there, and I clapped for him, and I laughed at the jokes, and then I think, "Am I a bad person? Am I supporting a predator?" You know what I mean? Does that seem silly to even think that? It crosses my mind.

Noam: It crosses your mind because you're a thinking person and there's this situation that's feeding us that we're supposed to think that way, but the fact is we know people all around us who have done bad things. I mean, if somebody at the table, the comedian table, said, "You know what, fifteen years ago I was in this hotel room with these girls," people would say, "You're a pig." No one would say, "You know, Noam, I don't think you should put that guy on anymore." We'd just chalk it off to another dude who did something disgusting, nothing to be proud of, but nobody would consider throwing him out fifteen years later. The world doesn't work that way. You wouldn't either, and then when he went on stage you'd be applauding, but now, it's just public now. And there's this whole thing around it. So there's this question of, "Is this okay? Am I doing the right thing?"

Author: And do you question yourself?

Noam: I did a million times. That's why I had reached out to so many people to speak to me about it, but nobody has any answers.

CHAPTER 201

The author speaks to Bonnie McFarlane,

Bonnie: I think Noam truly believes people should have a voice. That's how he books the club and that's why Louis gets to go on and that's why ... The other night I was with Hannah Gadsby and I almost had her convinced to come down to the Cellar and do a set, but she was worried she would run into Louis. I was like, "He won't be there," but when I got to the Cellar, Louis was on stage so I had to text her and say, "Hey, he's here." But I know Noam would have put her on.

Author: Why does she not want to run into Louis?

Bonnie: She's got a lot of Louis material I think.

Author: So it's because of that?

Bonnie: Yeah, and I think there's a misperception that the Cellar's saying, "Hey, we love this guy," when really that's not what Noam's saying. Noam's saying, "I give a voice to all these different ..." He would never tell anyone ... Ted Alexandro did this whole set about Louis and Cosby and the MeToo movement and stuff, and it went viral. Nobody was like, "Hey, don't do that, we're trying to get Louis back in the game." Noam just wants the discussion I think. I think Noam is really, truly coming from a place of his own belief system. He's not like kissing anybody's ass or trying to help anyone in particular. He's just, like, "I like when all voices get heard and all points of view get heard."

Author: I think there was concern from some people that having Louis at the Cellar meant it wasn't a safe place for female comedians. I wondered if you'd heard that?

Bonnie: I don't get it. I don't get that comment. Like, a safe place in what way? In that he's just going to whip it out and masturbate in front of you? I don't think that's going to happen anymore. That's bizarre. That's ridiculous. That's insanity. That's insanity. If a female comedian is sitting around scared Louis is going to masturbate in front of her, that's insanity. The thing about it being a safe place or not, that audience has already been curated for twenty, thirty, forty years. I don't think Louis coming in and doing sets is going to suddenly, "Oh, now it's a bro audience." It's always been a bro audience. That's the problem with the whole system. The system has curated this bro-type audience and now they're like, "Oh, women don't do as well." This is any club by the way, not the Cellar, any club, maybe any club in the world, I don't know, but in New York for sure. A certain type of person stopped coming to the club, and people who like sort of dirty, misogynistic comedy do come to the club. So when a woman or a minority gets on stage and they don't do as well, people point to it, "See what I'm saying? They don't do as well as these guys." That's because that audience likes that kind of comedy so much more. That's why they keep coming. So I don't think Louis coming to the Cellar is going to change. It's not making it worse. It is what it is. The soup has already been simmering for twenty-five years.

Author: I went to a lot of shows at the Cellar last week and Nikki Glaser did jokes about a vibrator and there were lots of women in there and they were laughing really hard, harder than they laughed at any of the other comedians.

8

Bonnie: There you go.

Author: And Liza Treyger told me male comedians complain about female audiences being terrible, but they're her best audience because she's telling jokes for them, whereas the men neglect them as audience members. Do you feel that?

Bonnie: I feel like that has been the issue from day one. Men tend to think that if they think it's funny it is funny, and if they don't think it's funny it's not funny, and nobody else gets to have a say in any of it.

[After twenty-two minutes]

Author: It's really hard because they won't speak to anyone really now since the *New York Times* piece.

Bonnie: Well because that's the thing, Louis gets to walk around going on stage, and they get death threats.

Author: Yeah. I saw Louis doing four shows back at the Cellar last week.

Bonnie: How was he?

Author: In the first one I saw, which was his third show back, and don't say this to anyone, but in the first one he was a real mess. He seemed really angry and he wasn't funny and I actually thought … Quite a few people left and I thought he might be about to clear the room. I thought everyone was just going to get up and leave, and he would just be on stage by himself. It really felt like that could happen.

Bonnie: He was on last?

9

Author: Yeah, he went on last. And then on other shows he was put in the middle, so it was harder for people to leave. So he was doing terrible, but then he did a later show that night and he didn't do some of the more angry stuff that he'd done at the beginning, and the next day he was much, much better, where he just kind of self-deprecated a bit about losing lots of money and stuff, and then he kept doing that each night for about three minutes. He'd do stuff like that, which wasn't really talking about the thing, just about the impact on him, and then he'd go into the jokes.

Bonnie: It's really too bad. He's so insightful. It's too bad that he can't be insightful about this.

Author: I was in the room and I clapped and I laughed at some of the stuff he said, but he was doing lots of sex jokes, and as soon as he was doing the sex jokes it pulled me out of it. I felt awkward, because your mind just goes straight back to, "Oh yeah, he's the guy who did that stuff, and here I am in a room kind of supporting him by laughing and clapping." I didn't clap at the jokes but I clapped him on and clapped him off and it's like … I think he's going to have a problem with that.

Bonnie: Did anyone boo him or anything?

Author: Nobody booed, but in the first couple of shows people left, maybe like a dozen people left in the first show and they weren't happy, but nobody booed. In one of the shows people stood up to clap. Maybe like half a dozen people stood up to clap for him.

Bonnie: Like, giving him a standing ovation? My god.

[After twenty-seven minutes.]

Bonnie: The thing you were just telling me about his set, maybe that's his penance? Now Louis gets to feel like what it is to be a female comic. Like, people kind of hate you when you get up there. You've got to really prove yourself. You can't do too much sexual stuff, you know? It's like, "Oh, look at you not having the easiest … Just get up there and be funny Louis." That's what comics love to say. "Just get up there and be funny." Well, now you know what it's like to have baggage.

CHAPTER 200

Before that, Louis CK goes on during the 11.30pm show. It's his sixth spot back at the Cellar. There's a loud roar. A sign on the wall says,

Anyone using any recording or photo device will be asked to leave immediately, no arguments, no second chances. Thank you.

The only camera belongs to the Comedy Cellar.

It records to a disk in a locked cage upstairs.

The cage is monitored by another camera.

The video will not be leaked.

Louis tells jokes. Some are about sex.

Nobody walks out.

Four men stand up and clap.

CHAPTER 199

Hours earlier, Louis does a spot during the 9.30pm show. It's his fifth spot at the Cellar since he took time off to listen. Half a dozen comedians watch through the doorway at the back of the room. Four people walk out.

CHAPTER 198

The night before, Louis does his fourth spot back. A few people walk out.

CHAPTER 197

Hours earlier, Louis does his third spot back. He says it's been a weird year. He says he's not a rapist, but he accepts the right of people to call him a rapist. It's a joke. He says the world has gone nuts. About a dozen people walk out.

CHAPTER 196

Days before, Louis sits at the back table of the Olive Tree, Noam's Middle Eastern restaurant on MacDougal Street in Greenwich Village. The Comedy Cellar is in the basement downstairs. There are steps down to the Cellar from the street or from inside the Olive Tree. The back table of the Olive Tree is a kind of green room for the comedians at night. A sign on the table says,

This table is reserved for Comedy Cellar comedians only. Thank you.

Louis is at the table having lunch with Noam. Louis asked for a meeting. It's the first time they've spoken in person since the story in the *New York Times* last year.

The author asks Noam about the meeting,

Noam: I don't want to talk about the meeting, but no he was not angry, he was just clearly overwrought.

Author: Because of what was happening to you or the club or because of what his life was?

Noam: I just think I really don't want this personal meeting between me and Louis being described in any way other than when I saw him it was clear to me that he had been through a lot, that's it.

CHAPTER 195

Author: I was looking on Twitter for the reaction to Louis coming back and there was one person who was quite sensible. She said that the Comedy Cellar should just put on a show with Louis advertised for that show, and sell tickets for that show.

Noam: But we can't.

Author: Why not?

Noam: Because people would show up to disrupt it. People would buy tickets and they would heckle. I understand the temptation to kind of defend these people and this trend of being uncivil and throwing people out of restaurants and pointing people out in the street and, you know, heckling at college campuses and whatever it is, but it's an ever-escalating thing, and it has downsides. I would love nothing better if we lived in a different culture where people didn't do that. They could strongly disagree but they would draw the line at disrupting a show that people had bought tickets for, which is not crazy. We probably did have a culture like that at one time. Then, yeah, we'd put Louis's name up and he'd perform and even people who were protesting outside it would be one thing, but now it wouldn't be that at all. For sure somebody would buy tickets or multiple people would buy tickets and they would come down and they would try to disrupt the show, and we can't take that chance. And somebody could get hurt. You don't know where that would lead.

Somebody next to them says, "Shut the fuck up, I paid money for this thing, go fuck yourself," and all of a sudden a punch is thrown.

CHAPTER 194

The author interviews Liza Treyger,

Author: So one thing we talked about when I spoke to you outside the Village Underground last year, and this was before the Louis CK *New York Times* story came out, so we talked about … You went and did *Horace and Pete*, and you said you'd been in the Cellar one night, you were talking about smoking, I don't know what you would call it in America exactly, but marijuana, cannabis, and Louis said not to do it because it would rot your brain, but because that stuff hadn't come out at all you didn't mention any of that other stuff, but the other week on the *YKWD* podcast you said this really interesting thing, which was when you were offered that part it did cross your mind that Louis CK might end up wanking in front of you.

Liza Treyger: Yeah, of course.

Author: That's amazing though. So, like, I guess I'd never heard a woman, a female comedian, say that. I'd never heard anyone say they were worried about that.

Liza: I don't know if I was worried. It was a thing that was known about him. Everyone knew and that's what all my friends asked me when I was like, "Holy shit, I'm going to be working with Louis." Every single person said, "What are you going to do if he takes his dick out?" Every single person. People didn't ask, "Oh, what's the part? What's the show? Where's it airing? Who are you working with?" The first thing anyone said was, "What are you going to do if he takes his dick out?"

CHAPTER 193

Louis does his second spot back at the Cellar. He's not on the advertised line-up, but Noam's added a note to the reservations email which is sent to customers,

Swim At Your Own Risk: We never know who is going to pop in. If an unannounced appearance is not your cup of tea, you are free to leave (unobtrusively please) no questions asked, your check on the house.

Noam's also put a sign on the front door,

Swim at your own risk, we never know who is going to pop in.

The author asks Noam about the new policy,

Noam: No one's going to be a captive audience. Anyone who wants to leave can leave and they don't have to pay, and anyone who stays will learn something about Louis in terms of how he wants to handle it, and they can draw their own conclusions about this famous man based on what he does or doesn't say.

CHAPTER 192

Weeks earlier, Noam speaks to Louis on the phone. The author asks about the call,

Noam: I contacted him through a friend of a friend to say I wanted to speak to him.

Author: On the phone?

Noam: On the phone yeah.

Author: How was it?

Noam: It was fine, he was nice.

Author: Did he apologize?

Noam: No. What he said was, "Noam, I love you," and this is almost a direct quote, "And if it's not good for you or the club that I perform there anymore just tell me, I won't come in anymore and I will still love you just as much as I love you now." That's what he said.

Author: How do you know that's a direct quote? Did you write it down?

Noam: Well it's pretty memorable. It's only a couple of days ago and it's a pretty memorable phrase coming from Louis CK. He and I have never really had many conversations ever, so … And that's not exactly verbatim, but it's almost verbatim, it's definitely the … Where he said, "And I'll still love you just the same." You know, he used the word love and he offered not to come anymore if it was better for me, and he made it clear that if I asked him not to come it would not change the way he felt about me personally, he wouldn't be angry.

Author: How did you react?

Noam: I said, "Look, I would hope that you speak to the people around you who are closest to you and you trust most, and gather all the advice that you can about what's the best way to do this. And once the best option becomes clear that's the way you should do it, but I'm not going to tell you not to perform anymore. I just want to make sure it's done in the best way." I said, "This is from your point of view Louis, this is not about the world or anything like that, it's like, you want to come back, so from your own point of view you want to do it in the best way that you can."

Author: Did you talk about the sign?

Noam: No, no, I thought of that afterwards.

Author: Right. So now your goal is to get the message through to his friends to get them to advise him.

Noam: Yeah, I hope it's the people that … This is the thing, nobody who I know who cares about him, and I speak to people who are close to him, think that, "No, no, it's fine." Everybody believes he'd be better off handling it slightly different, so you would hope that his friends would tell him so, but the thing is, when you're that famous and that revered, it's hard for people to talk to you like that, it's hard for them.

Author: Even comedians who are his friends?

Noam: Yeah, even with those people. I believe so. So, you know, when I prepared myself to speak to him I made a decision. I said, look, I'm just going to speak to him like he's anybody, because I want to be able to, you know, have my piece. I told him what I felt. I'm going through a lot because of this guy. A lot.

CHAPTER 191

Before that, Mike Yard introduces Ted Alexandro. Ted used to open for Louis. Ted walks onto the Cellar stage. People clap,

Ted: But what's with this PC culture? It's suffocating right? Do you want to live in a world where a man can't politely ask a colleague if he can take off all his clothes and masturbate to completion? Is that where we are as a culture?

Ted talks about President Trump,

Ted: Donald Trump said when you're famous you can grab them by the pussy and nothing will happen. Louis's version of that joke is when you're famous you can ask them if you can jerk off in front of them and clearly nothing will happen. Oh god, but there's people, right … Oh, but he's lost … He's lost … He's lost everything. It's not fair that men should lose everything in a flash, and by everything I mean hardly anything, and in a flash I mean a decade later.

Ted emails Noam to say he's putting the set on YouTube. Noam replies,

Don't worry about me. I don't expect anyone to hold their tongue.

CHAPTER 190

Before that, Noam receives tweets from @DanaAndJulia. The tweets say he's been trying to poke holes in their story and it's painful. They describe what happened with a headliner who masturbated in front of them in a hotel room and what happened afterwards. Noam replies that he never tried to poke holes, he just wanted to learn about it, and he did try to reach out to them privately, but this isn't for Twitter, so can they email or call him? He says he's expected to take measures so he feels a responsibility to find out everything he can. Please call. They don't reply or call. He stops looking on Twitter. He deactivates his account. His stomach acid's going all the time. It's very upsetting, this horrible hatred,

Noam Dworman is a fucking sociopath

He has no clue that this will be the downfall of a NYC staple

supporting rape culture

the club was possibly a toxic environment

Just another asshole giving abusers a platform

Fire bomb the comedy cellar

His father Manny would be embarrassed

CHAPTER 189

Noam's father is dead.

Author: Talking about Louis's return, you talked to other people about that, did you ever think about what your dad would have thought of that?

Noam: Yeah, I felt he would have done exactly the same thing. I asked Ava and she said, "Absolutely."

Author: Really? Where did you ask Ava?

Noam: That I remember. It was here. She was over at the house during the summer.

Author: Sitting around the island in the kitchen?

Noam: No, in the backyard.

Author: And were you sitting at a chair or something?

Noam: Yeah, just at that table you can see. I asked her what she thought. She was supportive and I said, "You know, Ava, I think my father would have been proud of this and would have done exactly the same thing," and she said, "Absolutely, no question about it."

CHAPTER 188

Noam's written about around the world. He tells the *New York Times*,

I think we'll be better off as a society if we stop looking to the bottlenecks of distribution — Twitter, Netflix, Facebook or comedy clubs — to filter the world for us.

He tells the *Hollywood Reporter*,

Listen, we are really a free-expression outfit, so let me digress and say that I've heard and seen comedians who work for me engage in real vile anti-Semitism, and I've never thought I would book them less or even said boo to them. I always felt this is their business. I don't have to like them, and people should not take me allowing them to perform as my approval of their character or the things they've done in their lives.

He tells the BBC,

I was worried about the reaction, you know. We're living in a time now of a kind of call-out culture where if you do or say the wrong thing people look to get even with you, so I was very worried. I am worried.

He records four podcasts about Louis.

Author: Why did you not just say no comment?

Noam: Because I thought that would have made me look bad, that I was being cowardly about it and, I don't know, I think people would have been more angry to see me not even ready to take responsibility for it.

CHAPTER 187

Before that, Noam wakes up at home. There's a text on his phone,

Louie is here and he's going on

It's from Val, a Cellar manager. She sent it last night. There are no follow-up texts. Noam asks Liz, the Cellar's general manager, to send the video. He sits in his pyjamas and watches. Louis doesn't talk about what he did. He doesn't talk about his time off. He tells a joke about a rape whistle. Noam tells Liz to delete the video at the Cellar.

Noam: As soon as I saw it, I said, "Oh shit, this is not going to be good."

CHAPTER 186

The night before, Louis does his first set back at the Cellar. As he walks onstage the crowd cheers and claps. The cheering continues as he puts his notes on the piano. It continues as he scratches his head. It continues as he takes the mic out of the stand.

Louis: Thank you.

The cheering continues as he takes off his glasses.

Louis: I know there's some people out there going, "No, no, no."

People laugh.

Louis: That's okay, I get it, that's how I feel a lot of the times, when I wake up and I look in the mirror and I'm like, "No, no mister, I don't think so."

People laugh.

Louis: It's very nice to be here, I took some time off because I just thought, you know, "I just want to relax a little." I had been working really hard and I thought it would be good to take some time off. It's a beautiful summer. It's been a beautiful summer. August is hot. I'm just trying to … this is, this is … I'm a little scared, it's a little scary.

A man in the crowd: We're glad you're back.

Louis: Thank you, I appreciate that, it's nice to be back.

People clap.

Louis: I'm really glad to be back too, at the same time I'm scared, so it's like, I'd rather … I don't know … I'd rather be in Auschwitz right now in a weird way, but not … I mean Auschwitz now, not in the forties. I mean now, when there's a Starbucks.

He tells jokes.

Some people laugh.

Some don't.

CHAPTER 185

Hours earlier, Louis does his first stand-up set since the *New York Times* story was published last year. It's at a club called Governor's on Long Island.

CHAPTER 184

Author: So between the time of that story being published in the *New York Times*, his film getting pulled and all that stuff, you hadn't spoken to him and then he showed up at your club one night?

Noam: Right. Correct.

Author: And then you said that you'd discussed … You said that you'd been thinking about this a lot in that time, between those two events, you knew it was going to cause you problems, and I think you said you'd talked to a lot of … I can't remember how you described them, but clever people, about what to do. I just wondered who you'd been talking to about this?

Noam: I can't say because they're going to get in trouble, but I spoke to some important liberal intellectuals and some important liberal figures in comedy, male and female.

Author: Okay. So you talked to comedians and you also talked to commentators, as in people who write opinion pieces for major newspapers like the *New York Times* or whatever, or *Wall Street Journal*, something like that, but major newspapers, yes?

Noam: Yes. Big names. Big names.

Author: Big names, okay. And what feeling had you got back from that?

Noam: Everybody felt that although I was in a very tough bind, that my arguments were correct. Everybody. Nobody was defending Louis based on what they felt they knew about what he had done or hadn't done, but nobody felt that I was obligated or that it was something that we would like to see happening in the country, that employers were now obligated to take measures against people who have a story in the *New York Times* and the employer has no ability to research it, and it's not involved in his work place, and it's fifteen years ago, and the person has admitted it … The problem with Louis is he admitted to certain parts of it but he didn't admit to the worst parts of it, you know.

Author: Okay. So when you were talking to these people, this was you working up your own argument, poking holes in your own argument, trying to get your argument as strong as possible so you could figure out if you would have a leg to stand on when he did eventually come back?

Noam: Correct.

Author: So this was about whether you should allow him back in the club or not, which I think you'd kind of decided that you would allow him back, but you just wanted to have the moral argument set.

Noam: Or somebody would convince me that I shouldn't, which wouldn't have been a bad outcome for me.

Author: But nobody did?

Noam: The only argument that they could come up with was expediency, you know, it's just, like, easier for me if I don't. But I didn't feel I could do that. I wouldn't have felt good about myself, especially with a guy who was figured into the place. I felt I owed him. I didn't owe him loyalty of letting him play there, but I owed him loyalty not to ban him because I was a coward.

CHAPTER 183

Noam writes a new draft of his argument and emails it to a friend,

We are all living in a hostage video. When James Gunn was recently fired as the director of Guardians of the Galaxy, *even his defenders were careful to point out that his jokes were "indefensible."* [Noam links to a story on *The Daily Beast.*] *They say it because they have to, I doubt they mean it. If Gunn's jokes are indefensible, then the Comedy Cellar is indefensible. Every night, tasteless jokes are told, and the audience roars. I'd love to give examples, but I don't want* [to] *clue the mob. Suffice it to say that virtually every comedian, even the very famous and beloved ones, have told more than a few Gunns. They're jokes. Devices. Even as kids we heard dead baby and Helen Keller jokes and we instinctually knew the difference.*

But I understand Disney too. They're in the kids business. They can't have a guy telling pedophile jokes (although they were quite comfortable with Roald Dahl) [Noam links to a website about Roald Dahl and anti-Semitism]. *They did the math and it was easy. Just like Netflix who apparently fired a man for using the n-word in a conversation about sensitive words — it's just not worth the risk. Today you probably can't quote* Pulp Fiction *in a conversation about whether to show* Pulp Fiction. *It's not deep principle, it's self-preservation, and who can blame them? (Even priests routinely close ranks to protect their own, I imagine selfless acts of principle are pretty rare among CEOs.)*

People are learning to shut up, and it's not just jokes, it's opinions. Many of the best comedians are philosophical contrarians but are now afraid to be too honest (again I can't give examples). A recent study found that fifty-eight per cent of Americans admitted to holding views they are afraid to share [he links to a Cato Institute study]. *Based on experience, I think that number is probably closer to one hundred per cent. At the Cellar, at our back table and various podcasts, we host many journalists, academics, musicians, and other prominent people. Every journalist I've met has an opinion he can't share at the office. Every academic has something they'll say only when the mics are off. Everybody's a phoney.*

It feels great to be outraged. Studies of drug addiction teach us about the "reward pathway" of the brain. It's activated by pleasurable experiences such as eating, sex, receiving praise. You can add righteous indignation to that list. If rats could feel it, they'd keep pressing that bar until they starved to death. We crave indignigasms (indignation + orgasm). To make matters worse, research has found that even as people have fewer things to be upset about, they are biologically programmed [to] *redefine new ones into existence* [he links to a story on *Science Daily*]. *It's as if we look at societal issues through a microscope and just keep doubling the magnification so we'll always have something ugly to look at. And we always react to it the same way — oblivious to the extreme magnification.*

This is all terrible for our societal health. We all have a lot of thoughts. Some may be insightful, and some may be horribly wrongheaded. But what we don't necessarily have is the capacity to tell which are which. To figure that out we might need to share those thoughts with others. Get feedback. Be dissuaded. But today, saying what you think, or even what you used to think, is just too risky — unless you're Joy Reid or Sarah Jeong, in which case the laws of gravity no longer apply.

But I don't think Jeong or Reid should be fired. Maybe Jeong is using "white people" simply to mean the Establishment. Okay. I'd like to see what she has to say about it. That's a column I'll look forward to. The habit today is to attack the bottleneck of distribution. The network, the newspaper, Facebook, Twitter. They are expected to fire people, censor them, ban them. Why not just let people say what they want? You'll live.

There's a civics lesson we seem to have learned lately a bit too well: the Bill of Rights does not apply to private behavior. But that technicality should not become an excuse. If the logic that inspired our Civil Rights is sound, then why shouldn't it apply in our private lives as well? It's time to reread John Stuart Mill. It's time for us to decide: Je Suis Charlie Hebdo or not?

Take Alex Jones. He's being banned from Facebook, YouTube, iTunes etc. Why stop there? Let's pressure the ISPs to block him. And if that doesn't work, why isn't tweaking the First Amendment the logical next step? What good is locking the door if the windows are still open? Enough with the capillaries, let's go for the jugular.

I'll tell you why. Because the censor will always get it wrong. The cure will always become worse than the disease — and quickly. The Times *had a piece recently describing how immigration has brought surging anti-Sem-itism to France* [he links to a story]. *My first thought was, imagine if someone had tried to warn of this outcome fifteen years ago. Would it pass Facebook censors? Would it have been called hate speech? This mentality is a cancer. It spreads to the notion that employers have an obligation to make hiring and firing decisions based on someone's private behavior, the jokes they've told, and maybe even for what they think (if we can unearth them expressing it somewhere). It validates the logic of trigger warnings and micro-aggressions. It's all inextricably linked. It's all the same faulty premise. I hate to say it, but there's an intersectionality to all of it.*

As with free speech, private citizens do not have an obligation of Due Process. But there's a layman's term for due process: it's called "fairness."

And there's a lot to be learned about everyday fairness by studying procedural due process.

As an employer, I don't want to be judge and jury of peoples' private lives. I can't compel testimony, I can't punish perjury, I don't have a forensics lab. I'm going to get it wrong. As soon as I start wielding my power as a club owner to punish personal behavior, I'm going to quickly find myself becoming a hypocrite — just like the New York Times *and MSNBC. We have a civil and criminal justice system to punish people.*

People always ask for instance if Louie will be able to perform at the Cellar again. My answer is yes. And hold on a second! I'm not endorsing or even tolerating anything Louie did. But what's the standard I'm being asked to follow? If I found out that a bartender did such things fifteen years ago, should I fire them? I remember when we once hired an ex-con with a violent past, people admired us for our progressiveness. Mike Tyson was the toast of Broadway. Okay yes, Tyson did his time, but how does a lesser transgressor get a new start? Louie hasn't worked in a year, is it supposed to be forever? I know of no crime that is punished with career capital punishment. The Comedy Cellar is just not the institution for such decisions. Buy a ticket or don't.

I talk a good game, but I fear that if the mob comes for me, I'll blink. I have a family to support. Other clubs have already suffered boycott movements for much less. We need to change the culture. We need a spirit of the Bill of Rights informing our everyday decisions and demands. We need to refute bad ideas in public.

Part of the joy of living in this country is being able to make up my own mind about things. At any given time, the greatest of people can see only inches above the heads of their contemporaries. To expect anything more than incremental progress is totally unrealistic. History will show that we are all getting it wrong most of the time — so let's not be so sure of ourselves. I don't want to be protected by some elite sitting at the bottleneck of my content.

There are good reasons to want to hear Alex Jones other than simply because you agree with him. We need it out in the open. Pushing it underground where the outrageous claims and statements are kept within a bubble only allows this stuff to take root. Conspiracy theories spread just fine prior to Facebook. At least on Facebook they can be openly challenged with facts. We talk the talk — "sunlight is the best disinfectant" — are we afraid to walk the walk? It was a good thing that Roseanne's tweet came out. Would it really have been better if a bot had prevented it and we had never known? Don't we learn from all of it?

I love this quote from Tyler Cowen: "As a simple rule of thumb, just imagine that every time you're telling a good versus evil story, you're basically lowering your IQ by ten points or more. If you just adopt that as a kind of inner mental habit, it's, in my view, one way to get a lot smarter pretty quickly. You don't have to read any books. Just imagine yourself pressing a button every time you tell the good versus evil story, and by pressing that button, you're lowering your IQ by ten points or more."

Mill said: "But the peculiar evil of silencing the expression of an opinion is, that it is robbing the human race ... If the opinion is right, they are deprived of the opportunity of exchanging error for truth: if wrong, they lose, what is almost as great a benefit, the clearer perception and livelier impression of truth, produced by its collision with error."

All I'm saying is please leave the Comedy Cellar out of this.

CHAPTER 182

Liza: I was sitting at the table a few weeks ago and an older comic came up to me. He was like, "You have to admit, young girls are the worst audience members. You have to admit that." It's like, why are you talking to me? And no, I do jokes for them. They like me a lot. That's my core audience. You're an old dude. Are you doing jokes for these girls? Are you catering to them in any way? And then you expect them to laugh at shit when you don't even acknowledge them? And you think they are the worst for not laughing at jokes that aren't made for them? So I'm like, "No, girls are the best audience for me and old white dudes are the worst."

Author: Is that true?

Liza: It is. They get mad at my material for sure. I have the worst trouble with dudes threatening to kill me, coming back to shows the next day, trying to ruin my bit, folding their arms. Like, dudes are the most upset because … That's what's the most annoying about all these white dudes claiming that MeToo's ruined everything and PC culture's ruined everything, is they're the most sensitive and they're the most offended and they're the most butt-hurt when anything is said about them. But it's like, I was just sitting minding my business, and I'm addicted to my phone, I was on my phone, someone just came up and said that to me. It's like, people just want to start shit with me.

Author: Who was the older comedian who said that?

Liza: It doesn't matter.

Author: Well I'm speaking to a lot of comedians. Would they get upset if you said their name?

Liza: Yeah, I'd rather not, it's like, honestly, they all annoy me.

Author: And also, you said three male comedians went up in the Village Underground one after another and complained about MeToo, and you went on after them. What was it that you said on the stage? How did you address that?

Liza: Oh, it was casual. The only thing I remember I said was just, "Hey, on behalf of all women, I'd like to apologize to all the men that MeToo has affected. I know it's been so hard on you guys." And then I just went into my material. I don't really know.

Author: And how did people respond to that?

Liza: Oh, like, applause break.

Author: Really?

Liza: Yeah. Sometimes when I'm like fourth or fifth in the line-up, and it's just dude after dude after dude, and I come on, you see women's eyes light up. They're so excited. It's like, they relate to me. They're excited to hear it. Especially because most of the dudes are doing jokes that are bullshit right now. So it's like, I can't imagine being a woman in an audience and three dudes in a row talking about how MeToo is hard for them. That's ridiculous. And that's another thing. All these dudes thinking that they're saying shit that's so edgy and counter-culture and look-at-me and it's like, no, you're the mainstream. Like, what you're saying is not unique. Oh, you think women lie and rape's not a big deal? Yeah, join the fucking world. That's the majority. That's what's annoying, these guys who think they're being edgy. It's like, no, racism is real and it's every day. You're not being edgy, you're being so common. You're being basic as fuck. And that's what they don't get. They think like they're being so cool by saying this shit and they don't realize that people hated women forever. You're not doing anything new. And it would be awesome to have a dude go up on stage … You know what would be edgy, to actually be like, "Oh, wow, dudes suck, we need to change." Like, that would be edgy.

Author: And is anyone doing that at the Cellar or at the Underground?

Liza: No, they think they do, but no.

Author: I really like the Cellar and I get on with Noam, and I'm quite honest with him I think, but it seems like there's an older generation of comedians there who want to keep the status quo where they can say whatever they like.

Liza: No one is stopping you dude from saying it, but audiences are allowed to not laugh. How dare you be entitled. You're not moving with the culture and people don't like what you say? What are you talking about? The Cellar's not stopping you from saying anything. Nothing is stopping you from saying anything. You can perform anywhere. You can do what you want. What are they talking about? People not laughing? Yeah, they don't like it. If all the women decide not to laugh at a domestic violence joke, they're allowed to do it. It doesn't mean they don't understand comedy and they're ruining comedy. They just don't like what you're saying.

CHAPTER 181

The author asks Jay Oakerson about being called in for a meeting with Noam. Jay tells the author he doesn't want to talk about it. Jay says he loves the Cellar. He says he told Noam he was disappointed that after fifteen years they'd call him in because a customer complained his jokes were racist. Jay says Noam quickly apologized about calling him in and told him to keep doing what he's doing and not change anything, which he didn't.

CHAPTER 180

Before that, the author phones Noam,

Author: I mentioned this when I was over, that you called in Jay, and I was thinking about that, because I really liked when you defended Sam Morril and you sent this email saying you can't decide what a comedian can and can't say on stage, which is why the First Amendment is so broad. But with the Jay thing, it's a bit annoying for me, because you called someone in, so there is a line.

Noam: Because it wasn't going over. There is no line. Sam said one errant joke and one person complained. It was an outlier incident. Jay was having a series of unhappy audiences. All I did was call his attention to it so that he could, if he wanted to, adjust. And by the way, I believe he did, because it stopped, so I don't even know what he's saying. I went down there the other night and saw Jay Oakerson and I couldn't believe it. I could not believe the level of filth that was coming out of his mouth, but we got no complaints about it. And I'm not even sure what he was saying in that little period. Sometimes when you say it to a person as opposed to generally, people are more likely to get upset. It can be very subtle. Jay's doing a high-wire act down there in the degree of filth that he wraps himself in, and his genius is in being able to present this stuff in a way which somehow people accept, but there was a little period there where all of a sudden they weren't accepting it like they always had, and I called his attention to it, and that's all I said. I said, "Listen, I'm just registering this with you, I'm not doing anything, I'm not affecting your spots, I'm not telling you what to do, but you need to know, because obviously you can't work if people don't want to see you," and that's, you know … He has a right to say whatever he wants.

Author: I guess from his point of view he'd say the room was laughing but there was one person in there who sent you an email, and maybe there'd been like an email before.

Noam: Yeah, but it wasn't just one email. We were getting a series of complaints about it. It wasn't just one email. I would never come to somebody about one email or whatever, unless it was something like they'd said, "You're a fucking cunt."

Author: So with Sam though, if Sam had got five emails about his alligator joke, you might have considered talking to him about that?

Noam: If he kept with that joke every night and we were getting complaints about it every night, yeah. I would say, "Sam, listen, what are you going to do here?" I would never tell him he can't do it.

Author: But it has a chilling effect on the comedian, doesn't it? Like, what I think Jay would say is it makes him wonder if he should or should not do a joke from then on, because is it going to stop him from getting booked at the Cellar?

Noam: Well, he may have to worry about that. I mean at some point that's up to him. He didn't get any fewer spots and he's still as filthy as ever so the outcome doesn't seem to line up with that having been something he had to worry about. Maybe at that meeting he was, but I tried very hard after that meeting, I even remember that night, I said, "Jay, I just want to make sure we're okay, I want to make clear I'm not telling you to do anything, I just want to put this on the radar because it's worrying me," you know, or whatever I said. But I mean, this is about the audience. I mean, it is. I don't care if the reason the audience hates a comedian is because he's bashing Arabs or bashing Jews. That would be me violating the free expression rule. But I do have the right to tell a comedian that, for whatever reason, whether it's just they suck or because they're dirty, whatever they're saying, "Listen, there is a clear and evident pattern here that this is turning off the audience." It's not about what he says. I don't care what he says. He can say anything he wants. I have to be able to tell him the audience is not accepting this.

CHAPTER 179

Before that, Leah replies to the Comedy Cellar feedback email,

I was extremely happy to see this email pop up asking for feedback because, yes, I have something to say.

I am SO upset by one of the acts that you allowed on your stage last night. It was the last act of the night — I think his name was A.J. His entire time onstage was spent making fun of gays for "blowing each other in the bathroom" and proudly stating that he "doesn't give a shit about politics." And while I can appreciate that those comments — while not really funny enough to warrant their stupidity — are his prerogative to joke about as a "comedian," some of this other content was SO completely disgusting and inappropriate that I almost walked out.

He talked about a couple doing anal in a hotel and how it was fine because "it would just be the Mexican cleaner's job to clean up all the shit in the morning." He then continued to push his fucked up joke by saying "here Guadalupe I'm handing you an extra $20." Not only is this moment in America a really fucked up time to be making jokes like that (does he read the news?) but his delivery and actual lines weren't nearly funny enough to warrant such a horrible choice in topic. He also joked about "fucking 18-year-olds," talking in depth about how he liked it when he got to hook up with those girls while they were really drunk and asking the host/MC if he would like to fuck drunk 18-year-olds as well. So he thought it would be funny to talk about potentially raping *and sexually assaulting young girls on stage. Cool. Again, perhaps a poor choice in topic.*

I appreciate that the point of comedy is to "push the bar" but I think we are past a time when men (or women) should be invited to get up on stage and joke about assaulting women. I think we are past a time when men (or women) should be invited up to laugh about immigrant workers when ICE is fucking up our country. The fact that you gave this guy a platform is incredibly fucked up, in my opinion, and I would expect more from one of the greatest comedy clubs in New York City. You have a responsibility to ensure that people aren't spewing more hate in the world. That really isn't what we need right now in this country, or anywhere for that matter.

I hope that this doesn't read as some holier-than-thou bullshit. I am not one of those psychos who writes long rant reviews on my Amazon purchases, but I was so angry about this that I felt I had to say something. I was also not the only one who felt this way, and the guest that I came with and MANY people around me were shocked and appalled by this pathetic comedian. He also just really wasn't funny, so even if his jokes were less offensive, he should probably just work on his general skill set.

Other than that, SO COOL THAT MICHELLE WOLF WAS THERE, and I had lovely service and thought the MC was great.

Thanks for listening, and I hope you never invite this loser back onto your stage. Perhaps even suggest to him that he reconsider using whatever influence he has and doesn't joke about sexual assault or rip on immigrants when our administration is making their lives a living hell.

CHAPTER 178

Noam: Nobody should ever get fired for anything they say, no matter what, and the only reason to fire somebody should be if, you know, people stopped watching or something. So, meaning like, if I found out that some comedian or someone who was under my thumb in some way said the most horrible things about Jews or whatever it is, I don't think I'd fire them, I'd just say it's not my business. I really do. It's too much. And what's so terrible about that?

Author: No, no, no. I think it's hard to say in absolutes.

Noam: I had a thing yesterday where somebody complained to me about Ann Coulter, because Ann Coulter made some really horrible remarks about the kids and Trump, and I actually emailed Ann. I told her what I thought about the remarks. That was private between us.

Author: Did she get back to you?

Noam: No, she didn't get back to me but she might or might not, but she saw it. But they're like, "You're not going to let Ann Coulter in now are you?" I'm like, "Yes, I'm going to let Ann Coulter in." This kind of thing … There's this expectation now.

Author: Who asked you if you would let her in now?

Noam: A guy who works for me. And there's an expectation that she's crossed the line, "You agree? She crossed the line? She's done right? You're not going to have her in anymore?" I'm like, "No, I'm not going to cut someone off because they said something stupid or something I find offensive." It's just … It never ends, it never ends, and the standard will constantly shift.

Author: And partly in your mind there, when you're talking about a hostage video and stuff, and you're talking about giving people the benefit of the doubt sometimes or allowing people to backtrack, or giving forgiveness, is it partly because at one point you feel it might happen to you?

Noam: Yes.

Author: Because I think that sometimes. This could happen to me. Someone's going to find something that I wrote or tweeted or texted to a woman ten years ago or something and it'll come out.

Noam: I mean, I'm not … I don't have a constant fear of it, but yeah, it's something that concerns me, only because if somebody's upset with me for whatever reason, let's say they didn't get spots, it's not beyond them to put a tape recorder … put an app that records on their phone and try to lead me down the path to saying something that they can then take out of context. And I'll never be able to wipe the slime off of myself. Even if I survive, it's there forever, and your great-grandkids will see it when they want to search their family tree.

Author: So you're quite careful about what you say in the Olive Tree now then?

Noam: Not as careful as I should be … It's hard, you get carried away.

Author: Well I mean, that's why it's oppressive, because you have to constantly live in this fear that someone's going to film you doing something or record you saying something, and it's not a good way to live. So you said that you had Milo in there? I heard that podcast that you both did, Sherrod's *Race Wars* one, and I guess that's why he came down to the Olive Tree is it? To sort of say hello or something?

Noam: Yeah, well, I was upset about Milo coming in, not because of his views, but because he had been very cruel to Leslie Jones. She was very hurt by it, and she's a member of the family, and I felt that … Now, I wouldn't throw him out if he had come in on his own, but I didn't think it was right that Sherrod invited him back.

Author: Oh, did Sherrod invite him to the Olive Tree?

Noam: Yeah, and I actually left as soon as he came in. I didn't want to be seen. That's just a personal thing about Leslie. I think it's ridiculous that anybody would care if Milo eats in their restaurant, wherever it is, but this is different, it is a personal friendship and it was personal to her, and I have to worry about having my friend's back in a sense.

Author: How did people react to him being in there?

Noam: Nobody really seemed to notice. He came with his husband, a nice-looking black man, and it passed.

Author: Did you comp Milo?

Noam: No.

CHAPTER 177

Judy Gold: That kind of material sometimes gets ... You know, if I mention the Holocaust ... It's getting worse and worse. It's really bad. And it's upsetting.

Author: Do you change some of the jokes that you're going to do?

Judy: No, never.

Author: Have you ever been telling jokes at the Cellar and people heckled?

Judy: Yeah, yeah, yeah, but you know what, I think more in the old days. Now, you fuck with a comic, you're out of there. That's the other thing I love about that club.

Author: What sort of stuff did people complain about? Did anyone complain ... I know that you didn't talk about being gay, onstage, for quite a while. I think you started talking about it in the Nineties?

Judy: Right, the mid-Nineties. I sort of came out as a gay parent. Once I had kids and I had all this material and I was like, "Come on, I've got to talk about my family in my act." I was gay, but I didn't want to be pigeon-holed as a gay comedian, I didn't really have anything to say about it in my routine. And here I am, I'm a mother, and what does it tell my kids if I say, "Listen, I'm not going to talk about this onstage"? It's like there's something wrong with that. But any comic who starts a family, their material changes. Their point of view changes. What they talk about changes. And what they think about changes. And the way they see the world. Their point of view changes. You see it from another person's eyes.

CHAPTER 176

Wil Sylvince is onstage,

Wil: Everybody was like, how do you feel about what Donald Trump said about Haiti? But I was mad when he said that shit about the Mexicans. What? Do you think when he said that shit about Mexicans, I was like, oh, but he feels different about Haitians? He's going to let us stay? Right? No, you go out too motherfucker.

CHAPTER 175

There's another Cellar debate. It's about free speech on college campuses. The moderator is Kmele Foster. The panelists are Jonathan Haidt, Suzanne Nossel, Jeffrey Sachs and Andrew Sullivan. Andrew makes an opening speech, which Noam records and puts on the Cellar's YouTube page,

Andrew: I want to try and draw back a little bit and look at this from the perspective of where I come from academically, which is in political thought. And I think that part of the crisis that we are dealing with is a conflict between two visions of the world. And the vision of the world that is in the ascendant is one that has always been the norm in human society throughout history. And that is that fundamentally you are a member of a group. And that groups compete for power. And that in fact everything in our society is really a function of these power structures. And these power structures used to be defined in classic Marxism as classes. Economic classes. Currently they are more often defined in terms of identity, things you can't help that you are, or things that you're proud of that you just happen to be. Your race. Your gender. Your sexual orientation. Your gender identity. And the view is, and you can feel it not just on campus but everywhere, that our society is basically a function of the oppression of some groups by other groups, and that therefore the most important thing to figure out is who is oppressing whom, and the most important thing to do is to resist the powerful or the more powerful and to defend and protect those with less power. And the power is a kind of invisible thing, because it's not purely class, although class is mixed up with it. It is about how one feels about oneself and how one feels about other people. And so the most powerful group, and you can hear this in the rhetoric every day, are white, straight, cisgendered men. They are the ultimate oppressive force, and you can go down, and there's a hierarchy, and we could have all sorts of complicated ideas about who's where in the hierarchy, but essentially that's what our society is, it's a constant fight between these groups of people. And in fact because as a society we're becoming more and more diverse, the intensity of that fight is growing. We are and will be the first white majority country to become a non-white majority country in the history of humankind. These are very powerful psychic effects. And in those circumstances, and especially with incredibly divisive and polarizing political parties, we're beginning to see our entire society and culture governed by which group you're in, and your ability to represent that group, or to betray that group. And the notion that these groups have fixed interests and certain ways of thinking that distinguish them from one another. This essentially draws its roots in Marx, but also in the critical theory schools which are now taught as simply the truth in most universities. So we're concerned if there are too many white people on a panel. We're concerned if there are too many men. We're concerned if there are too many straight people. And speech affects power. So because this is so amorphous, if you say something that makes an oppressed group feel more oppressed you're not just speaking, you're actually harming those people. Speech is not simply a way in which you are discussing things. It has immediate impact. It has harm. It commits harm against groups. It is a power play, and there is only power in this view of the world. All rhetoric is simply about defending your power or about seizing power for yourself. We are a tribal species. This comes very naturally to us. The history of humankind is really in many ways a story of these struggles between these groups. But there was an experiment in human history, beginning sometime in the seventeenth century, of which this country is the ultimate product, which says that no, no, no, no, no, this is not what we are. We are actually individuals. We have our own selves and we construct our societies to defend ourselves as individuals not as groups. That we therefore recognize, for example, freedom of religion as a fundamental right, because no group can tell you what to believe about the universe. We represent and defend private property, because private property is a way in which the individual is protected from the group and the mob. And we believe that when we're trying to figure out the truth in a society, the way we do that is argument, we use reason. And it doesn't matter whether you're white, black, pink, purple. Whether you're gay, straight, trans, bi, queer, asexual, you know, the rest of the alphabet. What matters is simply the cogency of your arguments. That's all. Have you made a good argument? Have you persuaded someone or have you not? And power is really less important than truth. And when you become a citizen of this republic you're as equal as anybody else, and your opinion is worth something regardless of whether you're a man or a woman, or black or white. In fact, those things are kind of left behind when we become simply citizens. I became a citizen recently of this country, and I wasn't ...

The audience claps.

Andrew: Thank you. It took a long time but I got there in the end. And I didn't become a gay citizen. I didn't become a white citizen. I didn't become a Catholic citizen. I didn't become an English-American. I just became a citizen. And my voice has no more power and no more validity than the strength and cogency of my arguments. Now, those two ideas are in direct conflict, and the forces of the group over the individual are immensely powerful right now as society goes through enormous demographic change. And what matters, it seems to me, is that in that process individuals both in the minority and oppressed groups, or in the oppressor groups, are allowed their own conscience, allowed their own voice, and are treated no better and no worse than anyone else. And that's the conflict. Are you to be treated as simply the member of a group? Is your activity on a campus or in the wider world really a function of power? Or are you an individual capable of making up your own mind, sometimes bucking your own group, saying what you think, and having that being taken seriously on its own terms without being called to account for being a gay person or a straight person or a white person or a black person or all the other characteristics that accumulate onto us. That's what's at stake here. The silencing of individuals. The intimidation of individuals by those groups. The loss of imagination and understanding of our society as really one of equals and individuals rather than groups. And power. That's really what's at stake. And that's why this is not just a crisis for the campus. It is a crisis for the general culture. It's a crisis whereby you can find people on the Right and the Left slowly being purged from positions of influence or from positions or platforms that they otherwise might have, because they're violating the group norm, because they're saying something the group doesn't like, or because they're acting as if they have a right to say something when in fact because they are white and male, or because they are black and female, or whatever, they don't have a right to say what they think in that particular circumstance. Those two visions are at war right now. You can see it everywhere. You can feel it. You can feel the air and the oxygen in most of journalism and culture becoming … having a little less oxygen. People being more likely to be called racist, sexist, homophobic, bigoted, blah, blah, blah, blah. And in fact, that being the main argument that people use in rebutting other people's arguments. And that is what I think we need to resist, and that is what I think we're in danger of completely surrendering to.

CHAPTER 174

Guy Branum writes an article for _Vulture_,

At the Comedy Cellar in Greenwich Village, there's a table where the comics sit. It's where they joke, debate, goof off, and ridicule their friends. As depicted on the FX series Louie, _it's the most fun place to be with the smartest, coolest comics in America. Every club has one, but the Comedy Cellar is the best club, and the table Louis CK sat at was the best table, occupied by the likes of Chris Rock, Jerry Seinfeld, and Marc Maron. That table is the most important force in comedy. There are rarely women at that table. There are never gay men or trans people._

I'm a cisgender man, thus not someone who has had to deal with sexual harassment of the sort Louis doled out to his colleagues. But I am a gay man, so I understand very well the kind of culture that harassment helps enforce, and which is perpetuated by that culture.

Here's a New Yorker _article from a few months ago about the table_ [he links to it]. _It lists seventeen comedians, including, of course, Louis CK. Only three are women, they are confined to a single line of the article. None are gay men. The article defines the table as sanctified space, reserved only for the realest comics, and discusses their hostility to even minor changes to the table. The article describes how these comedy icons "defended the table against comedians who didn't do stand-up at the Cellar, were hacks, or were dressed badly." People who weren't like them didn't get to be part of the club. I am not like them. Louis's victims were not like them._

61

That boys' club is the only real structure that exists in stand-up. The patronage and mentorship that good comics receive from more established male comics is how they get stage time, representation, and jobs. Improvisers and actors have schools and casting workshops to help them build skills and connections, but for a stand-up, you're always just waiting for one of the guys — and it is always a guy — to pay attention and help you out. If you're not part of their club, you learn that such mentorship rarely comes your way, and when it does, it often has a cost.

Sexual harassment is one of many tools heterosexual men use to remind other comics that our status is provisional. We're not equals. We're not colleagues. We're flavors, we're different, we're people who should quietly accept whatever creepiness is presented to us. Mostly, these tools remind us that our status as real comics is provisional. We understand that if we question the rules of the table, if we say there aren't enough women getting stage time, or that maybe they shouldn't use that word, or even just that Kesha is more talented than Springsteen, we'll be expelled.

Louis, of course, sexually harassed numerous comics. He was not expelled. When managers, club owners, and comics became aware that he was assaulting comics, they did not say, "Hey, let's figure out what's going on," or "He might be a threat to the other comics." They protected him. They made the problem go away. They kicked Megan Beth Koester out of the Montreal Just for Laughs festival.

That's because Louis's behavior didn't hurt the system. It maintained the system. It alienated women from careers in comedy and allowed everyone to continue to live in a world where they could believe that the table, the Official Council of American Funny, was a place only straight men were worthy of reaching. Louis CK once said during a Daily Show *appearance, "Comedians and feminists ... are natural enemies." The table doesn't have any space for comedians who are feminists.*

I'm scared to write this, because I know the people who sit at the table will see it and say I'm not a real comic, and I don't value real comedy. Writing this means I never get to sit at the table. At the beginning of my career when I was invited into some lesser comedy boys' club, I did my best to play by their rules. I kept silent as they denigrated women, or explained to me how I wasn't like the other gays. It never earned me real respect from anyone, least of all myself. My silence simply empowered a system to treat me and many other people like we were negligible and disposable.

In more recent years, I've questioned the established rules of comedy, particularly as they relate to discussion and participation by gay comics. Once I did a TV segment mocking the homophobia of a Comedy Central show. A famous, respected, politically liberal comic unbooked me from his show because he didn't think comics should criticize other comics in public. He never considered that when the Comedy Central show in question was incessantly ridiculing homosexuality with no gay comics present, they were criticizing those comics. They were criticizing me.

So that's why I'm writing this, so I no longer have the option of sitting at that table. We don't need a female comic with provisional status at the table. We don't need the table to find the trans comic who's least offensive to them and kind of learn his name. It will still perpetuate a system that privileges and protects the perspective of straight cis men. The table is the problem. Burn the table down.

Noam leaves a comment online beneath the article,

I'm the owner of the Comedy Cellar. This is libellous. Can you back up your description of the Comedy Table in any way? It's total fantasy. A total lie. The precise exact opposite of the truth. Do the right thing. Admit you made a mistake and take it down. Or lawyer up.

Guy replies in the comments,

The table is a metaphor, but ... Your web page has photos of fifteen comics, one is a woman, none are gay. Your photo album has photos of sixty-five comics, five are women, one is a gay woman. Tomorrow (11/11) your 7:00 show has seven comics, one is a woman, none are gay. Your 8:15 show has seven comics, one is a woman, none are gay. Your 10:30 show has seven comics, none are women or gay. Your 12:15 show has seven comics, one is a woman, none are gay.

Noam comments again,

Everything you have just written may be true. Unfortunately what you wrote in the article — that there are rarely women and never gays — IS NOT. We put on the best show we can. How many openly gay comics, Cellar level, do you think there are right now? You've never submitted a tape. I actually watched you on YouTube at the table last night, and laughed out loud at your haunted vagina joke. I don't know if you're good enough for the Cellar but you've never even tried. We book the best show based on who is available. PERIOD. I couldn't care less if it's all female or all male. It usually works out in between. You accused me of sexism and homophobia. That is a baseless charge and I really will sue you if my lawyer says I can. I don't care what it costs. What you have written is verifiably false. Reckless disregard for the truth, I believe is what they call it. Or, just retract the parts which are wrong. Maybe you made a mistake. If so, don't be ashamed to admit it. Most would admire it.

Noam comments again,

Really, if you had any understanding of the Cellar, you'd realize it was the very opposite of what you decry. It's a place where the only thing anyone cares about is whether you're funny. Like the NBA, can you score or not?

Guy receives an email inviting him on the Comedy Cellar podcast. He replies, saying the Cellar's threatening to sue him and *Vulture*, but he'll come on if Noam waives all claims. Noam says okay. The *Vulture* lawyers write a contract. Noam signs it. Guy is a guest on the Cellar podcast at the back table of the Olive Tree. The podcast's co-host is Dan Naturman. Rich Vos and Rick Crom are also guests,

[After six minutes]

Noam: Are you ready to say that it's not true that gays are never at the table?

Guy: At this literal table, of course there have been gays. The thing I am ...

Noam: At the Comedy Cellar?

Guy: This week you guys have Mehran Khaghani performing. The thing that makes me saddest about everything that I wrote is the fact that it did not respect or contemplate the place of Jim David at this club or on *Tough Crowd*. Like, having a gay man in stand-up comedy ... There are currently no gay touring national headliners.

Noam: I'm talking about my club here. I could not care less about anything you say about ... I might agree with you. There's plenty of bigots in the world.

Guy: The only thing I was saying about your club is that it is the apex and it is reflective of that ...

Noam: No. Why?

Guy: Because it is on *Louie*, because it is the representation of the comedy community ...

Noam: Hold on, hold on.

Guy: That you saw on *Louie* and that was an article …

Noam: On *Louie* …

Rick: That's fiction.

Noam: Hold on. No. No. There's a better answer than that. On *Louie*, when he depicted the comedians … Alright, it was at the poker game rather than at the table, but it was the same group …

Guy: Right, it was at the poker game. That is the only time that Rick Crom showed up on that show, and when he stopped teaching Louis a lesson he went away.

Noam: But it was …

Rick: I did three of them.

Guy: Okay, I'm sorry.

Rick: We did three poker table episodes.

Noam: And it was a huge event in the gay … It got a lot of attention as being one of the …

Rick: It was.

Noam: Most sensitive portrayals of … And it was credited with stopping stand-up comics from using the word "fag" in their acts, all because of that thing that came from the Comedy Cellar.

Rick: Which was something that Louis asked me to do when I saw him here at the table. He said, "I want to put those stories that you've said here at the table on the show and I want to reflect how we all are supportive of one another." We bust each other's balls, but at the end of it I'm still part of it, I'm still one of the crowd. So in that scene, not only is there all this information, there's also this great camaraderie and acceptance that I think should be reflected in any ...

Noam: Was that reflective of the Comedy Cellar?

Rick: Yes.

Noam: Listen, this is how I fantasized this show would go, that you would come here and you would acknowledge, "You know what, you're right, I shouldn't have said that about the table, I should have been clear I didn't mean the table," whatever you meant. And I figured, oh that'd be great, and then we could launch into a bigger discussion of the things that are important to you, which are how women are treated, how homosexuals are treated. But it's very important to me that you clear my name, or if you don't want to clear my name, you don't have to, that you back it up with some facts.

Guy: I have asserted that I'm not claiming that this club is any better or worse ...

Noam: You keep doing that. I don't care about any other club. You said that this table never has gays. Never. Is that true?

Guy: No, it is not true.

Noam: Okay. This table rarely has women. Is that true?

Guy: Again, I feel ... No. And I feel ...

Noam: Okay, that's all I wanted to hear.

[After fourteen minutes]

Noam: I just want to let you know something, at five years old I used to be taken to dinner parties with gay couples. Gay male couples. My father and my grandmother would take me to socialize with gay male couples at five years old and I knew and understood … They told me exactly what it was and my whole life has been like that. This place in the Sixties was known to be accepting of gays, as a place where gays could come and work and didn't have to hide, before anybody was like that. What you have done is attacked the very people who are on your side.

[After thirty-seven minutes]

Dan: Well, I challenged him on Twitter, because he also made the point that there's no transgenders that work here, to give me the name of a transgender. He did give me such a name, I forwarded it to you, I don't know if you want to look at her.

Noam: Of course I'll look at her. By the way, is there any transgender host on MSNBC? I mean, transgender, really? If I don't have a transgender comedian working here that's evidence that I discriminated against transgender?

Guy: Not you, comedy as a whole.

Noam: What percentage of the population is transgender?

Guy: I have no idea.

Noam: Well you need to know these things before you make statements.

Guy: But I know that Patti Harrison is a really good comic. I know that Riley Silverman is a really good comic.

Rich: Have they been on your TV show? Have they?

Guy: No.

Vulture changes the article. It now says,

There are rarely women or gay men at that table. There are never trans people.

Noam receives an email from an editor at the *Vulture*. He replies, saying the article still maintains the table seldom has women or homosexuals, and it maintains that the Cellar is a sexist bigoted outfit, and it maintains they protected Louis. He says those things are not true and he would be happy to debate it with an editor.

CHAPTER 173

Before that, an article appears in the *New York Times*. The headline is,

Louis CK is Accused by 5 Women of Sexual Misconduct.

Noam: Nobody knew. Nobody knew. We all saw the rumor on *Gawker* and some people had heard the rumor, but nobody knew as a matter of fact. Louis I think had denied it to the people that he did have a close enough relationship with to discuss it and they believed him, so no, they didn't know.

CHAPTER 172

The author interviews Kevin Brennan after he's called a racist by a woman in the audience at the Cellar. The author's already interviewed the woman,

Author: I said to her, I think it's a funny joke. Do you not use it anymore?

Kevin: It works all the time. I stopped doing it because it was an older joke, and then with the whole Trump stuff, there was definitely backlash when Trump was elected and there's backlash now, period, where if you're a white comedian, white, male, not young, and you basically have any kind of an attitude, they associate it with, you know, anything, like the MeToo thing, any kind of aggression, any kind of testosterone or I-don't-give-a-shit kind of an attitude, they take that as you're potentially dangerous to them, so they have to yell.

CHAPTER 171

The author interviews @9amburritos, who called Kevin a racist,

Author: I can understand people like yourself who are very outspoken about, you know, ensuring there's progressiveness. I can understand you guys becoming more ... And I'm kind of left and liberal, but I'm not as outspoken as people like you ... I think I can understand why you become more defensive about it all now, and police it more, because you can see the wider stuff that's happening in society. Is that correct? You can see the Trump thing happening, so you're thinking, well, I can't do anything about Trump, but I can do something about this stuff in front of me?

@9amburritos: Yeah, right. Because in that room there was a lot of bystander effect going on. Like, I shouldn't be the one. Diffusion of responsibility, you know? It's like watching an accident happen, like watching someone hurt in front of you. Who's going to ... It's not my responsibility to say ... And I wasn't even the minority that was being attacked. I think I would have flipped out even harder if he was talking about Asians. But I think there's a lack of empathy that is happening, because there is so many things to care about now, to be upset about and ... I don't know, I think people are just exhausted, empathetically exhausted. And I forgot to say this, but after I heckled, a woman who I think was sitting at the same table, but her back was to me, she turned around and was like, "I'm an Arab and I'm okay with that joke." She said that, you know. That just made me so sad.

[After thirty-nine minutes]

@9amburritos: I think a lot of what the older generation of comedians is scared about is, "Where's the line? Like, if I can't talk about this then what can I talk about?" And I think it's all about doing it in an intelligent way. And another thing is, what they say is, "It's just comedy, it's just a joke, it doesn't mean the person is racist, it doesn't mean the person is sexist," but I think that having the platform to say something and to have people laugh at it, I think it makes the thing you say socially acceptable. Like, if you say something and the crowd laughs at it, the audience, they look around and they're like, "Oh, this is socially acceptable." And I think this is kind of analogous to the presidency in a way, because when Donald Trump first became president people were like, "He's just one guy, it's not going to change the mindset of American people," but it did just that.

Author: You said in one of your emails that it was a kind of green light to people to talk a certain way and show certain attitudes.

@9amburritos: Right, so when Kevin Brennan, someone who's paid to say things onstage goes up there, says something, the crowd laughs, maybe there's someone in the crowd who goes, "Hey, that's a chill thing to say, so I'm going to start saying that, so that's an okay thing to think," even though it's presented in a joke. So I don't think it matters whether someone is inherently a racist. I think it's what you put out there that matters.

CHAPTER 170

Before that, Noam emails @9amburritos,

I'm Noam Dworman the owner of the Cellar. I'm just finding out about this now. I will talk to Kevin and see if I can have him stop this Twitter stuff. People are especially disgusting with anonymity provided online. Kevin's material is not PC, but honestly he's not a racist. His wife is dark-skinned Hispanic, which I know is not the end of the story, but it's not irrelevant. The jokes are kind of in character, like Archie Bunker.

Most of the comedians, from the most famous on down, have some material that some find offensive and over the line. That's the nature of comedy and comedy clubs. I don't control their material, nevertheless I don't take your reaction lightly. Interestingly, there is some material that is done that I find offensive, that I notice seems to go down ok with the audience. It's not as easy a call as you might think.

I'd be very happy to have you back as my guest on a night when the line-up is more to your taste.

@9amburritos replies. She says the Cellar shouldn't book comedians like Kevin and she hopes New York businesses will be on the right side of history.

Noam replies, repeating his invitation to return to the Cellar as his guest, but adding that he would never be able to define an acceptable joke,

So sometimes I wince and wait for the next act.

CHAPTER 169

Before that, @9amburritos writes a message to her friends,

It all started when I was at a stand-up comedy show at the Comedy Cellar in NYC on September 4. I live in Brooklyn and I frequent these shows. This time, however, an incredibly racist comedian was perform-ing: Kevin Brennan. He was second to go on stage, and his entire set was based on racism/sexism.

First, he called a girl in the front row "titties" then he said "it's okay, I'm married, to a guy" like being gay is the punchline. Then he said he got stopped on the subway because he had a backpack on for a random check, which he was mad about because "I can't be a terrorist, I'm not an Arab" THEN he pointed out a POC waiter and said "that guy looks suspicious, he's wearing a backwards hat so he could blend in" and then he said "it's okay, I can be racist because I have a Hispanic wife."

People laughed awkwardly, or perhaps in agreement. But nobody said a thing while Brennan was spewing unfunny HATE SPEECH on stage. Simply because he was on stage. The couple beside me whispered "We really don't like him." But I'm sure many people in the room thought, "I would never be brave enough to say such a thing. Good for him!" Which was the most disappointing part.

I, being the enraged liberal I am, heckled him, calling him out for being a racist. I was promptly kicked out by the bouncer. I shed some angry tears, but was overall okay with the repercussions. To me, it was worth it. I couldn't stand it if he went on uninterrupted. He called me "sweetie" on the way out and made a joke out of me. This was normal for him.

I went home and sent a tweet outlining what I did, and that I didn't regret it and that white comedians don't just get to do whatever they want. What I didn't expect was that the comedian Kevin Brennan would retweet it. That was when I started receiving hate mail from his racist fans saying that comedy is sacred, calling me racist slurs and harassing me daily. It got even worse when another more famous comedian friend of his, Jim Norton, quote-retweeted me chastising me for my actions, clearly looking to send his angry, racist and bigoted friends my way. I started receiving hundreds of tweets and DMs calling me sexist and racist slurs, insults about my appearance and intelligence. Anything in attempts to hurt me. When my friends came to my defense, they too were quote-retweeted by Norton. He had one goal, to hurt us with his 500k following, almost all of which were MAGA right-winger white men. You can probably find many of these just by looking at Norton's tweets and replies to them.

CHAPTER 168

Before that, a friend visits @9amburritos. They go to the Cellar. Kevin Brennan comes on. He does his joke about a cop searching his backpack, where he says to the cop, "I look like a terrorist?" And the cop says they have to randomly select people, so Kevin says, "Well randomly select Arabs." The cop says, "Sir that's racist," and Kevin says, "That's okay, I'm racist." @9amburritos hasn't heckled before, but when Kevin says that joke and all the other things too, she shouts. A bouncer asks her to leave. She leaves. She cries. She tweets comedians to tell them what happened. She tweets to her followers,

yelled at a racist comic at @NYCComedyCellar tonight and got kicked out. I regret nothing. White men don't just get to do whatever they want.

Kevin retweets her tweet without a comment.

Jim Norton retweets it with a comment,

I agree, you have every right to interrupt a live performance, those other paying customers are NOT important, YOU need to be heard.

People tweet to @9amburritos,

you not smaht for chinky

you're a fucking slant-eyed moron

shut your mouth you slant

we'll be clapping as they hall your ass over the border #DACA

we'll be laughing our asses off while you're kicking and screaming

#deport

It gives her flashbacks to when she arrived from China as a kid. She responds. She gets banned from Twitter.

Author: What did you get banned for?

@9amburritos: I don't remember. It must have been like the "I hate white men" thing.

Author: You said that?

@9amburritos: I don't like saying it, but in that moment I think I said, "I hate white men," and I'm sorry.

Author: Do you hate them?

@9amburritos: No I don't.

CHAPTER 167

Anthony Cumia's drinking in the Olive Tree. Jon Stewart's in the Olive Tree. Jon shakes hands with people, but won't shake Anthony's hand. They argue. Noam asks if they're okay then walks away. They shake hands. It's written about. Noam writes a statement which is published on the *Interrobang* website. It includes the line,

disagreements in good faith are normal and healthy

CHAPTER 166

The *New York Times* publishes a story about a Cellar show which happened on January 11, 2017. Most of the advertised line-up was bumped and the line-up became Jon Laster as emcee, Ryan Hamilton, Dave Attell, Jerry Seinfeld, Amy Schumer, Chris Rock, Aziz Ansari and Dave Chappelle. The headline in the *New York Times* is,

A "Billion Dollars' Worth of Comedians" for $14 and a 2-Drink Minimum

CHAPTER 165

Author: So that night, January 11, 2017, you were hosting a show that ended up with Seinfeld and all those people on. Did you know it was going to be a big show?

Jon Laster: I think a lot of people have this misconception about what was happening. Val was the manager that night, so when I came in we knew that just the opposite was going to happen, that they weren't going on.

Author: So you knew they were up here but they weren't going to go on?

Jon: We knew that they weren't going on. When I walk in the line-up is there, but the manager kind of tells me what's happening when we have people here, so she basically said, "Don't worry, here's the people that aren't going on." So they definitely weren't going on. To let you know how much they weren't going on, I did all my time up front. Ryan stayed on the show and did all of his time. There's no way they would let us do that time if we thought all of them were going on. First of all, they would have cut Ryan, they wouldn't have let him go on. But they weren't going on.

Author: Do you remember what phrase Val said?

Jon: Yeah, she said Amy was around the corner hanging out with

Colin Quinn. She wasn't going on. Chappelle wasn't going on until the next show for sure, and she said maybe Seinfeld would go up and maybe Chris, but the rest of them definitely weren't, and we didn't think that we had time for them. It was throughout the course of the show that all of them decided, "Hey, I'm going to go up," "I'm going to go up."

Author: So you went up, did your time as a host, then Ryan went up, did his time. Did you know at that point it was going to be a different show?

Jon: No, no. The trigger was Dave and Chris were downstairs talking. Amy had come downstairs ...

Author: Dave?

Jon: Dave Chappelle and Chris Rock. And Chris is kind of like asking Dave, "Hey man, which one of us is going to go up next?" And Amy overheard them and said kind of like, "Fuck that, you guys are going on? I'm not going to miss this." Schumer's going to the bathroom. She was just walking through the conversation. So then she basically said, "Hey, can I do five?" What am I going to say, no? She turned around and said, "Can I do five?" So then once I put Amy up, that's when the dam broke.

Author: Okay, so she goes up, and then you're in the hallway at that point?

Jon: Yeah, because you can't light them, so I've just got to wait until everybody gets off stage, but fortunately, that's when everybody kind of started looking around, "This is about to turn into something." Everybody's being respectful, they're getting off stage pretty quickly, you know what I mean?

Author: So they didn't do long, did they?

Jon: No. Chris did some time. By the time he got on, he did some time.

Author: So Amy went up and then just said, "Right, ready to come off"?

Jon: Yeah, yeah, yeah, she was like, whatever, whatever.

Author: Did someone say to you who was going to go up next?

Jon: Yeah. Then Val was saying, "So and so's next, so and so's next."

Author: How did you feel at the end of the night?

Jon: Oh, man, it was surreal. I knew that there's no way there could ever be a show that came together like that which was bigger than that. There's no way. There's no way you could have that many people that could fill up Madison Square Garden on the same show. No one's ever … I knew no one had ever seen a show like that.

[After eleven minutes]

Author: When you were sleeping on a train, a few years before you were passed at the Cellar, what train was it?

Jon: Oh man, I used to sleep on the 2-train.

Author: Did you have a sleeping bag or anything?

Jon: No.

Author: So you just went and sat on the train?

Jon: And nod off as long as you can.

Author: I've seen people doing that, it looks horrible.

Jon: Oh yeah, brutal. It was brutal.

Author: How long did you do that for?

Jon: Three weeks, yeah, probably.

Author: How did you get out of it?

Jon: I decided to check myself in.

Author: You checked into a rehab?

Jon: Yeah.

Author: Can you do that for free?

Jon: Yeah you can.

Author: Where did you go?

Jon: I went to Kingsboro, a place called Kingsboro, a rehab centre in Brooklyn. Yeah.

Author: So you got off the train and went there and said, "Look, I need to fix my life"?

Jon: Yes.

Author: Did it work first time?

Jon: No. No. I had to go a couple of times.

Author: Did you go back to the same one the second time?

Jon: Yeah.

Author: How long was it between the first time and the second time?

Jon: Oh god, maybe six weeks. Maybe.

Author: Oh, because there's one time when you came out and went straight to the liquor store?

Jon: Yeah.

Author: That was after the first time I take it?

Jon: Yeah.

Author: What did you buy at the liquor store?

Jon: Vodka. More vodka.

Author: Oh man. That's amazing. Thanks for talking to me, Jon.

Jon: Yeah.

CHAPTER 164

Before that, the line-up for the 9.30pm show on January 11, 2017 is Jon Laster as emcee, Ryan Hamilton, Dave Attell, Hasan Minaj, Judah Friedlander and Michelle Wolf. Ryan finishes his food and goes on. The crowd claps politely,

Ryan: I feel like I just disappointed everybody. I just felt the whole crowd go, "Oh no, this guy, I don't even know who he is. I was going to give him a chance but we don't know him. We don't. Where's Louis? Where is he? Where's Chris? Where's Jerry? We don't know him." Well, you're going to get what you paid for right now.

Ryan does his spot. He goes home. He's got an early flight to Atlanta. Dave goes on, but the rest of the line-up gets bumped. Jon goes back on. He tells the crowd not to record videos. He introduces Jerry Seinfeld. Jerry tells the audience he doesn't care about video. He says to the audience,

Jerry: "They're so special and what they're doing is such magic. We can't let it out of the room." But it's not. It's nothing. It's jokes. We're doing jokes.

CHAPTER 163

The author writes an article for the _New Yorker_ about the comedians' table being moved. Noam hates it. He tells the author it reads like he planned to move the table, but it was moved against his wishes and he was fixing that error, so he didn't take a chance that failed like Colin's quote says. And regarding the new table, Noam says it's almost impossible to determine exactly where the table was before the renovation, but contrary to the quotes from Liz and Colin, it is back in the same spot.

Noam: The whole thing is just stupid. Anybody who'd ever done renovation knows it's tough and you're tweaking things and you're figuring things out, and it's not done until it's done. And the idea that this was some sort of decision, you know, it was just absurd, it's not the way it happened at all. On the contrary it was always supposed to be not moving, the table. Period. That was always it. I mean George, my business partner, said, "Yeah, you said it over and over." It was the only part of the whole renovation I was really interested in. Like, "I don't know about kitchens, you guys can do whatever you want in the kitchens. Liz, whatever equipment you need, the answer's yes, the only thing I care about is that the table doesn't move."

CHAPTER 162

Before that, the author emails Liz, the Cellar's general manager. Noam told the author to ask her for any measurements. The author tells Liz that Colin thought the table's not back in the same spot it used to be. She emails back,

The table is MAYBE a few inches off from where it was previously.

The author includes the line in his article.

CHAPTER 161

Before that, the author phones Colin Quinn,

Author: Hello Colin you alright? It's Andrew.

Colin: Hello Andrew, how are you?

Author: Are you alright to talk now Colin?

Colin: Yes I am.

Author: Fantastic. Great. How did your physio go?

Colin: It's good, it's good, it's fine.

Author: Knee still?

Colin: No it's my Achilles, nine months ago, but it's getting better, but it never gets completely better they said, so it's over for me in many ways.

Author: Ah, no.

Colin: Where are the snows of yesteryear? Where are the snows of yesteryear?

Author: Um.

Colin: Um, so yeah, so the table.

Author: Yes, great, so this is a piece I'm doing for the *New Yorker*. It's not like a huge feature, it's just the Talk of the Town section. It was commissioned at eight-hundred words but I think it's going to, it was eight-hundred-and-fifty words when I submitted it, and they asked me to put some more quotes in, so it's going to be a thousand words or something like that, but the point of it is, it's about the history of the table a little bit, but the reason I'm writing about it is that ... So Noam took this decision to extend the kitchen in the Olive Tree, which seemed like a risky move to me, but he decided to do it and that resulted in moving the table. The table was moved around for a little while and then he had a permanent position for it, and there was, like ... Rachel Feinstein described it as a bit of a backlash against him having moved the table, and I think Chris Rock sat down and had a rant at him, and a couple of people have said stuff to him.

Colin: Hilarious.

Author: And so he paid $20,000 to get the walls pulled down again and get the table moved back. I think it's a really nice story.

Colin: Oh my god. A really nice story? Yeah, it's a really nice story, the extortion of Noam by the fucking comedians. What a story.

Author: I kind of laugh when I talk to him about it, but he can afford it, he's alright, I wouldn't laugh if it was, like, really putting him in a bad spot.

Colin: Oh my god, yeah, well I mean, you know, I didn't know anything about this part of it, because I've just been kind of MIA from that room for a while, I just haven't been going in, but I mean the table, it's funny, because Liz, you know Liz the manager, I was talking to her about this yesterday and she said, yeah the table, it's ... You're in the middle of everybody but you're separate, like you're there and you're not there, and that kind of was it, like, they didn't want a private room.

Author: Liz by the way, I wanted to know the dimensions of the table and Noam ...

Colin: She told me, she sent me the whole, yeah ...

Author: So Noam said, oh Liz will do it for you, and I was like, it was really awkward because I've never met Liz before, and then, it's like trying to ask her to do a favor for someone she's never met, but anyway, so she probably didn't think much of me, but yeah, exactly, I mean, I know that you hadn't been at the table for a while and I heard you say that the table was over, but for a period you enjoyed that atmosphere of being in the Olive Tree, being amongst it, but still having ...

Colin: Oh yeah, I mean, it's still a great place to sit down with people, you know what I mean, but as far as it being a bad version, a dumb version of the Algonquin round table, those days are over, yeah.

Author: People like Joe List and Mark Normand, they love being around it, you know, those sort of younger comedians do love it still.

Colin: Sure, yeah, I'm sure they love it now, it's their table, you know.

Author: I mean, do you think it was a wise decision by Noam to move it?

Colin: Do I think it was what?

Author: A wise decision for Noam to move it. To risk upsetting, like, Bill Burr said Noam ruined the whole aura of the place or something, and then Chris Rock kind of had his say, so people were clearly unhappy with the fact that he moved the table. I wondered what you thought, whether, you know, you thought that was …

Colin: Well I mean, I wouldn't … You know, the history of the table is very simple. Nick Di Paolo once said to Manny, there's no place to hang out in this fucking place, and the next day the table said for Cellar comedians only, so that's how it happened, that's how it began.

Author: I spoke to Nick and he told me about that, which was great.

Colin: Yeah, it's pretty interesting, so he takes full credit, as he should, because I was there when he said that.

Author: Were you?

Colin: Yeah, I heard him say it, in the litany of complaints that he had that night, that was one of the things that was thrown in. And then um, but I would say the table, I mean … I guess Noam … I didn't know … I wasn't sure where Noam moved it to. I guess he moved it out into the room?

Author: He moved it closer to the bar, which I think was a problem for people because … I think, like, Louis wasn't happy.

Colin: Right, because then everyone's looming over you, fucking harassing you. I mean, you know, and it's noisier I guess, because the table, it's like … There's a reason the Last Supper happened in a private room in the back apparently, because otherwise, you know, Jesus would have been like, "Listen, this is probably, you're not going to see much of me anymore," and somebody would have recognized him from the bar and said, "Jesus, you're Jesus," and he's like, "Yeah, yeah, I'm just, I'm in the middle of something," and they're like, "Jesus, I can't believe it," and he's like, "No, I just want to do this thing where I give the bread to the one guy that's going to betray me, it's kind of a serious moment." "Yeah? I love it, what are you guys ordering?" And he's like … You know what I mean? It would have ruined the entire, you know, climax to the second half of the New Testament.

Author: So, so, so you understand, you know, why some comedians wanted it moved back to where it was then? You kind of get that?

Colin: Yeah, I mean, sure, I mean, of course, only because, you know, if you're in the middle … I mean, there's a lot of famous people come in there and I don't blame … If you're standing next to somebody famous, I certainly did that when I was a young drunken dickhead, I would be like, yeah … Obviously it's got to have a little bit of a boundary to it. It doesn't have to be a VIP fucking velvet rope, we are comedians after all, nobody cares that much but, you know what I mean?

Author: And what did you think of his decision to kind of renovate the kitchen and start selling like steak and, you know, higher-end food?

Colin: I mean, yeah, I liked it, because it's like, nothing stays exactly the same, you know what I mean? You can't just keep going, hey … I mean, the shocking part is that since I started going there in the Eighties it's the same … All this renovation in the kitchen, all this renovation and everything … The bathroom is in the back of the room. It's small, uncomfortable, it's exactly the same as it was back in the Eighties. So it's like, we're sitting here, I mean, basically, you know, mowing the lawn while the fucking house is on fire, in my opinion, but it's like, yeah, go ahead.

Author: Can you describe the bathroom a little bit more?

Colin: The bathroom, it's part of what keeps the Comedy Cellar great. It's basically, you walk in the bathroom, you're wedged in, even the guys' room has a line, that's how bad it is, not just the women's room. The women's room goes halfway through the crowd. There's times when you're waiting in line for the bathroom, you're blocking the back table from watching the show and … But that's part of the charm of it all. And then the guys, you're lined up with a bunch of guys, you know, and everybody's just wedged in this corner, and one guy's … You literally, if you have any homophobic tendencies you might as well not go to that bathroom because you're going to be brushing against a guy while he's peeing, you're going to be right behind him, basically dry-humping him while he pees, that's just how it goes. So if you're uncomfortable with that, don't come to the Comedy Cellar. It's like a clown car, you know, and it's always in the middle of a show, so anybody walks to the bathroom, the comedian harasses them going there, and it's been like that since the Eighties.

Author: And it's kind of weird, because people are now going to be having this nice food, like, made by a proper chef up in the Olive Tree, but they then want to go to the toilet, they're still going to have to get, like, the code, and go through one of the shows, and go through to that bathroom downstairs, aren't they?

Colin: Exactly. It's absurd, but I mean, you know, that's how it is.

Author: Yeah, yeah. I want it to all just stay the same as it is, I don't want them opening up new rooms or anything, I just want to keep it as it is, but it's Noam's business and he's got to do what he's got to do, you know.

Colin: Yeah, it's like, everybody's like, hey, we want to be quaint, except the person that's … Really, you want to be quaint? You know, what I mean?

Author: But it also feels like there's … and I'm only going to be a couple of more minutes Colin, but, it also feels like there's important historical sites in New York and particularly in Greenwich Village, and it feels like that table was quite an important historical site within the entertainment industry, within stand-up comedy. Stand-up comedy is a New York thing and this is one of the most important spots within the whole world for stand-up comedy.

Colin: Oh, definitely.

Author: So it felt quite surprising that they'd move it, and move it around, and quite sad I suppose as well.

Colin: Well, like I said, it was all so … I mean, you know, the table itself, it wasn't … You're acting like it was some beautiful oak fucking master … It was just another shitty table that Manny goes, "Okay, Di Paolo's pissed, there should be a place for them to sit, he's right." I mean, it wasn't fucking Lancelot and King Arthur, you know, chopping down a beautiful, masterful oak tree and bringing it out of Sherwood Forest to build a table. I don't think they even did that. So it's like, it's more symbolic than the actual table.

Author: That's what I mean, it's the symbolism of it.

Colin: Yeah, it's a state of mind, you know.

Author: And do you think that can survive having been moved?

Colin: I mean, yeah. Look, we're comedians, we're supposed to be, like, these flexible people. Everybody's like, "What the hell's going on?" It's ridiculous, you know, what are we, in a private golf club in 1880?

Author: And I just wanted to run a couple of things that people had said past you. And I know that you're friends with these people, so I feel alright saying it …

Colin: I'll say if I'm friends after I hear what they said.

Author: Okay, yeah, sure, so Rachel Feinstein said she knew there would be a backlash. She was … This is all … It's a light-hearted piece, so this isn't them really criticizing Noam or anything like that.

Colin: No, I know.

Author: So she said that she, you know, would sit around the table and bitch about it, amongst everyone. Hang on a second, I'm going to read this out, so she said they would just bitch about it basically, the table didn't feel right, it felt weird and they didn't care for it one bit, but she knew there was going to … She knew that they were going to hear about it, meaning Noam and Liz and Estee I guess, and she felt confident that the backlash would be strong.

Colin: Right. Yeah.

Author: Yeah. Seems reasonable.

Colin: Well, I mean, that's what she said?

Author: Yeah, that's what she said. That's alright, isn't it?

.

Colin: It's fine, I mean, you know, I guess there would be a backlash at anything. I mean, comedians, we like to backlash, that's what we do.

Author: Yeah.

Colin: Our profession is to backlash, you know.

Author: Yeah, and apparently Chris Rock, so he wasn't happy with it and said this isn't the table where Ray Romano sat, this isn't the table where Robin Williams sat, this isn't the table where Jon Stewart sat, and Noam said each one of those was like a punch in the gut.

Colin: Yeah, and there's one other problem with that. When those guys worked the Cellar there was no fucking table. The table started in 1998, how's that grab everybody?

Author: Did it?

Colin: How about a little reality? How about we lose the mythology for a second? The table started in 1998. Ray Romano was already on his show, Robin Williams was fucking ... and Jon Stewart was doing his show.

Author: I'm going to have to rewrite my piece.

Colin: Ha ha.

Author: The, um, so Bill Burr ... Bill Burr went on Kevin Brennan's podcast, so this isn't a quote that I got from Bill Burr, it's something he said on Kevin Brennan's podcast, and he said, ah shit, sorry man, oh, he said, "What did Noam do to the table down here? He literally fucked with the whole aura of this place." I wondered what you thought of that?

Colin: That was what he said, yeah?

Author: Yeah.

Colin: Well I think people are being a little dramatic. I mean, I was in there when the other table was happening and I felt like it wasn't the same, but you know, it's better in the back now, it's better that it's back where it was, I mean in that back section, definitely, you know, but it wasn't the biggest catastrophe of all time, Jesus, everybody's making ... It's better where it was, but it didn't fuck up the aura.

Author: Right, okay. And then the last one was Robert Kelly and he just said ... Robert gave me some other great quotes as well, which I've used in this piece, um, and he said ... more ... more ... more comics could sit there but it wasn't the table. So to him, you know, it had fundamentally changed.

Colin: Well, I mean, well, it's fundamentally changed anyway. Here's the thing, it's not in the same spot it was in. Right now the new table is not where it was.

Author: Yeah. What? Why? What? What? The one where it is now?

Colin: Yeah, that's not where the old table was.

Author: Robert said that Noam had put it back exactly where it was.

Colin: No, it's not where it was. It's close, but ... It's in the same far end of the room, but technically it's not the exact spot, you know what I mean? And it's, um ... I like it better, definitely, I like it better.

Author: You like it better?

Colin: Yeah.

Author: Not than the original one?

Colin: No, but, um, actually, I do like it better than the original one, now that I think about it.

Author: Oh, do you? Okay. You're a great contrarian for this piece.

Colin: Well, I like the, um, I like the location better than the original one, you know. Yeah, but I mean, I feel like, you know, Noam is trying to update … It's like a comedian, "Hey, I liked your fucking … I liked your original act, what are you guys writing new shit for, it's not as funny. That first hour, that was the best shit." You know what I mean?

Author: Yeah, so you understand what Noam was doing?

Colin: Yes, he was doing what everybody … Yeah, of course, I mean, he was doing what everybody does. Noam took a chance. Everybody's like, "Whoa, whoa," but guess what? We do the same shit in our act, and sometimes it fails.

Author: Yeah, oh that's great.

Colin: You know what I mean?

Author: Yeah, that's an awesome line.

CHAPTER 160

Before that, the author asks Rachel Feinstein about the table,

Rachel: We get homesick. We text each other. We have these lifelines to each other, whether it be a picture of a dirty green-room or some crazy hotel. We send them back and forth with my best friends that are comedians, like Nikki Glaser and Schumer. So home, and that is our home, you just want it to feel like it's supposed to.

CHAPTER 159

Before that, Noam pays $20,000 to have the table put back where it used to be,

Noam: Truthfully, I am extremely sensitive to vibe and atmosphere. Extremely. Like, I walk into my place and I can tell you the dimmer is an eighth of an inch higher or lower than it normally is. I see a lightbulb that is out in a second. I knew. Nobody needed to tell me. I knew exactly what the problem was. I knew exactly how it felt. None of it was a surprise to me. The only thing I kind of waited to see was whether or not other people picked up on the change in the same way that I did, but it wasn't as if I ever sat there and said, "Oh, this is great." I always felt what it is that was wrong from day one, and I tried to see if there was a way to make it work by changing the bar, to try and fix it without having to spend the huge money that we had to spend to move the wall again, but in the end nothing really worked. And even if Louis and Chris hadn't said anything to me I would have known it wasn't good.

CHAPTER 158

Before that, Noam replies to Louis,

The original architect's plans had no move of the table. When we started there was a slight relocation. It's one of those things where no plan survives contact with the enemy. In any case, I won't quit until the problem is solved and I won't consider it solved until you're happy with it. I don't believe in luck. Hopefully we'll have food back in about two weeks. Thanks for everything. Please never hold your tongue with me. I'm going to fix this. I understand exactly how important it is.

CHAPTER 157

Before that, the renovation is complete. There's a new comedians' table. It's a few feet closer to the bar than it used to be. Noam receives an email,

Hey Noam. Louis CK here. I wanted to share some feelings I have about the current state of the Comedy Cellar. It's up to you to decide if it matters what I think because it is your club, but in either case here's what I think. I completely understand your reasoning for hiring a chef and therefore needing a bigger kitchen. That makes sense and it meets your needs as an owner. And I can see that a smaller back bar area is an unavoidable consequence of the bigger kitchen. The problem is that you've completely killed the comics' table. I cringe every time I sit back there. The table is butted up against the end of the bar. Last night there was a couple sitting in the two stools that loom over the comics' table and I sat there with Sam. Both parties were miserable. We could hear every word they said and vice versa. That's the problem when it's quiet. When it's crowded on weekends it's untenable. Everyone is on top of us. There is no safe place. Add to that the new policy that seems to be that customers wait at the bar area to go to the show room. They gawk at us as we eat our food. The outcome of this is that I hesitate to go to the club anymore and I absolutely don't go on weekends. I have plenty of weekend nights that I get restless and consider popping in but a huge, huge part of that past pleasure is gone. That we had that corner. As long as you survived the gauntlet of MacDougal Street, the crowd outside and the Olive Tree you were safe at the comics' table. That is no longer the case. Besides the fact that when I haven't had dinner I now choose between going to eat or dropping in for a set when I used to be able to combine both. That accounted for a huge amount of times I've done sets there. I know food is coming back but I am not eager to eat at that cramped little table two feet away from fifty fans or a couple trying to connect. Chris Rock has said these same things to me and he's even more upset about it. As he told me he told you, "you're lucky there's nowhere else." Whether you want to continue to rely on that luck is up to you. It seems to me that there are many solutions to this problem. If I were you I'd create a boundary, a new stronger boundary, and incorporate the end of the bar into the comics' area. Some comics like to sit at the bar when there's room. Maybe create a rope line at about the fourth stool from the back wall of the bar and give that tiny table more breathing room and just call all that whole space "comics only" bar and table. You might lose a little money but I really doubt it would be significant. That's up to you. Maybe you have a better solution or maybe you like it the way it is. Again, it's your club, which you don't need me to point out. I'm just giving you a data point which is that the current state of the club already has significantly lowered the amount of times I would have popped in since it changed and that my willingness to show up there continues to erode. How much that matters is your business. I love the Cellar. It's been a big part of my life for decades. I'm grateful for the love and support I've gotten from you and your family over the years. That's why I'm bothering to write.

Take care, Louis.

CHAPTER 156

Before that, Bill Burr's a guest on Kevin Brennan's podcast, *Misery Loves Company*, which Kevin records in Noam's podcast studio above the Olive Tree,

Bill: What did Noam do to the table down here? He literally fucked with the whole aura of this place.

Noam hears the podcast and texts Bill,

Yo, we moved the table over four and a half feet in order to double the size of the kitchen, so the fucking comics can have steak and pasta instead of falafel every night. Lol. I'll get the kinks out. Who likes to be criticized on material they're still working on? Otherwise, great show.

CHAPTER 155

The author interviews Noam about Chris Rock,

Noam: Why would he think we would get rid of the table? That didn't make sense.

Author: So it was a misunderstanding?

Noam: Yeah, nobody had warned him. He walked in, the place was being renovated, and you know …

Author: What do you do at that point? Do you get in touch with him? Or do you hope he comes back? Do you try to get a message to him?

Noam: No, I didn't. Actually, I probably should have. I just assumed that he'd find out right away that it wasn't true. And I mean, he speaks to a lot of comedians. Keith still comes … Everybody's been still coming down. Amy's been coming down, Ray Romano's been coming down, you know. I don't see it as … Actually, I think Chris was down, sitting at kind of like the makeshift comedy table a few weeks ago. I think he was.

Author: And I was wondering who made the biggest grumbling about it? I didn't know if it was Sherrod or someone like that?

Noam: By the way, who quoted it on the podcast, do you know?

CHAPTER 154

Before that, Mark Normand records his podcast, *Tuesdays With Stories*, with co-host Joe List. He says he bumped into Chris Rock outside the Cellar the other night,

Mark: Chris Rock was bitching. That's what we talked about. He's like, "This place is over. They did it to the Strip, now here." I'm like, "Well, they are changing it back. It's just temporary." But he's like, "Once the comics stop hanging it's done."

CHAPTER 153

Work starts on Noam's $300,000 renovation.

CHAPTER 152

The author phones Noam,

Author: So I was kind of thinking about, you know, you've taken over this business from your dad, you're expanding it, opening up new rooms. Your dad had created this ethos to the Comedy Cellar and the comedians appreciated that and seemed to have admired your dad in the way they talk about him now, it was obviously a big deal, so you're kind of taking on a lot, and you haven't restrained yourself and gone, "I don't want to change anything because if I change anything people won't like it," you know, "And then I'll be ruining this thing that my dad built." You've been brave enough to open up these new rooms, kind of have a documentary made and things, and the kitchen, you're changing the kitchen, so I kind of wanted to think about that a little bit, and how much your dad is on your mind when you do these things. The kitchen is the easiest one to start with. It seems daft to talk about a kitchen but it's just a way of illustrating something, so don't think that I'm madly obsessed with this kitchen or anything, but can you tell me why you're expanding the kitchen?

Noam: Yeah, well, the Olive Tree has always been a struggling business. When my father was alive, before the Comedy Cellar was as successful as it is now, and I had my music club the Cafe Wha, he was struggling to make money in the Olive Tree. The Olive Tree was always a low-cost place that had a limited menu and struggled with a small kitchen. And it took many, many, many hours of his time and emotion to keep the Olive Tree as a viable business, both watching expenses and quality control, and all these things. That is very, very difficult and I didn't want to get sucked into that, especially, especially, especially when I had my kids, because the Comedy Cellar is a business which doesn't run itself but allows me freedom. I can go away. I don't have to go to work every day if I don't want to. Much of it I can do back home. But the Olive Tree and any restaurant really requires ... Essentially there's something to be done every hour that you're awake and every hour that you're not at the restaurant is a compromise for every restaurant owner. So I didn't want to do that, and the only way out of that I could think of was to hire a chef, like a real kind of chef. In a famous restaurant the chef is kind of the guy who's responsible for everything to the owner, he's the guy who has to spend all the time, so we didn't have a kitchen which was big enough. I know it's a long answer.

Author: No, no, no, I'm after a long answer.

Noam: So I decided to expand the kitchen to make it big enough such that we can hire a real chef who can then take over the Olive Tree kitchen and essentially run that aspect for me. And will also allow us to have a ... I don't want to stop having reasonably priced items, but it'll also allow me to have things like steak or fish or some nicer items, and after all, the Olive Tree has a very important clientele as it is now. I mean, you know, famous people eating there all the time and they're eating falafel and hummus, so it would be nice to have some mainstream items on the menu. So then I ... But the truth is that my father and I thought almost one-hundred per cent alike on most things. And I know he would be thrilled with the idea of what I'm doing. This is nothing that he would even ... When he was alive we wouldn't have had the money to do it, or it would have been a big strain to do it, so he wouldn't have done it as easily as I did it, but right now that the comedy's doing well and I'm able to pay for it almost completely out of the money coming in, although I'm taking a loan for about thirty per cent of it, but that doesn't put a strain on my lifestyle as it would have ten years ago. So that might have stopped him from doing it, because we always lived hand-to-mouth for almost our entire existence.

CHAPTER 151

Lena Dunham sits at the table with Estee Adoram, who books and schedules comedians at the Cellar. Judd Apatow introduced them to each other recently. Judd's started doing spots at the Cellar. Lena's interviewing Estee tonight for her newsletter, *Lenny Letter*. Lena asks if any jokes upset Estee,

Estee: I hate vulgarity. I don't mind dirty. There's a difference between a comic who works dirty or is vulgar. I don't want the level of intelligence to go down the toilet because of that. I have personal stuff that I don't like. I wouldn't be offended, but I don't like it. I don't like Holocaust jokes. The only one that can pull it off is Dave Attell. He can do it and it works. I'm from a Holocaust-survivor family, so that's a very raw nerve for me. I don't particularly love cancer jokes. People do that. If you manage to do it where the audience laughs, I turn my head. Those are pretty much it.

Lena: How do you feel about rape jokes?

Estee: Depends on how you do it. You need to come and you're going to listen to Lynne Koplitz doing the rape joke. If you don't laugh, I'll buy you whatever you want.

CHAPTER 150

Author: How did you come to write that joke? Was that deliberate? You thought it's a subject you want to tackle?

Lynne Koplitz: I had a little paring knife under my bed. I live here in the Village, which is true, and I have for twenty-something years, and I was thinking, "I don't really think this would keep me from getting attacked." My bed was pushed up against the window and I watch a lot of *Law & Order* and I thought, "I wonder what would help me? I bet I could love him. What if you loved him? I bet that would really freak a rapist out if you just loved him." I don't have a really good streak with men, like, I've needy-ed and scared away men, and I'm like, "Hey, that's one thing I do well is freak out men. I bet I could freak out a rapist." And I thought about how I would do it. And I was at The Stand or something one night and it was literally like somebody's new joke night and I threw it out there, like, "You can't rape me, I'll kiss you on the mouth." And it got a huge laugh, like, way bigger than I expected. So I was like, "Woah, I need to write this." So I was thinking about it and thinking about it, and Estee and everyone will tell you, I don't write like other people, I'm an actress at heart, so I've always been like ... I watch and study and think and roll things around in my head and if I look at jokes it'll freak me out, so sometimes when I need help on a premise then I'll sit down and just, when the spirit moves me, I'll just power drive through it and write it out longform and then I'll come back and do it. I just keep ...

Author: On a pad of paper?

Lynne: Yeah on a pad of paper.

Author: So that joke came about over a year or two years?

Lynne: It was probably starting to form for about four or five months. And we were at Montreal, and I was friends with Joan Rivers, she was like a mentor to me, and we were on the gala together and, oh, that was the other thing, I felt I had gained all this weight and everything was changing for me, I was getting older and the jokes that had worked in my half-hour special just weren't working anymore, and I was on the road and I needed … And my TV shows were gone. I was getting ready to do the reality show with Joan and Melissa but I hadn't gotten it yet and I was like, I've got to figure something out. And I've always been good at being authentic I think. And believe it or not I pray a lot. And I just prayed to God and I was like, "What do I do?" And something said to me, "Tell them the truth."

Author: Something said to you?

Lynne: Something in my heart said, "Tell them the truth." And I went out on stage and I wasn't as pretty and I wasn't as skinny, and I was like, "This is what you look like when you start giving up." And it got a huge laugh and I said, "I don't know how funny I'm going to be but I'm full of information." And it got a huge laugh and I thought, "Well, I can work with this. This is better." So I'm going to Montreal and I do that and then I do … I close on the rape joke. And it wasn't completely evolved yet, it's way better now, but it had the rapist being the baby spoon, and it had putting baby kisses on his rapey hands, and it had the thing where I say, "I'm your girlfriend now." And I see Joan coming backstage across this mammoth gala stage with her assistant at the time,

Graham, holding her orange Birkin bag, and Joan's in this big fur thing that, you know, says Canada on it, it's a Canadian flag, like a little Liberace with the hair, and I can see her with her arms out, just walking as fast as she can across the stage, and she gets to me and she goes, "That joke, the last joke, who wrote it?" And I said, "I wrote it." And she said, "Did anyone write it with you?" And I said, "No." And she said, "You wrote that joke all by yourself? Lynnesy, look me in my eye." And I said, "I did." And she said, "It's a game-changer, you've got to get it on TV." And I said, "Well this is TV." She goes, "This is Canada." And it was so funny. And I said, "Thanks Joan." And she goes, "No, no," and she turned to Graham and she goes, "She doesn't get what I'm saying. Do you understand why that joke's great?" And I said, "Yeah, you know, it's a taboo topic." She goes, "No, no, no, no. That's not why. You took a taboo topic and you made it funny, that's what makes it a good joke, that's what makes you a comedian. You know what makes it a great joke?" I said, "What?" And she goes, "You made it request-able. People are going to request the rape joke. That, kid, that's a game-changer. I'm so proud of you." And then as she walked away I heard her say, "He's the inside spoon."

Author: So, have you done it on TV?

Lynne: Yeah a couple of times and now it's on my special.

Author: On the Netflix one coming out? Congratulations by the way.

Lynne: Thank you, like the long version of it is on my special because it has a short version and long version.

Author: When did you do it on TV?

Lynne: I did it on Dave Attell's ...

Author: Oh, *Comedy Underground*, the one he filmed here.

Lynne: Yeah, and again it wasn't completely developed.

Author: And when you started putting your address on it, when did that come about?

Lynne: Yeah, the *Comedy Underground* people freaked out because they were like, "We can't. Standards & Practices called and said we can't do the address."

Author: Is it your real address?

Lynne: Here's the thing, because I was doing my real address and they said, "We just can't, she can't do her real address." So I said, "Well can we do two doors down?" Because what I like is people in the neighborhood would see me in the neighborhood and think it was my real address. So the NYU campus is right here, the law school, so they got me a law school address, but then Netflix said, "No we're not even going to do the law school address." They freaked out and said, "You can't even do that." So on Netflix I basically tell them that Netflix won't let me give the real address but that I live near a coffeehouse on Sullivan Street.

Author: Is that recorded then?

Lynne: Yeah.

Author: And when you do that joke and give your address, it works best in the Cellar or Village Underground doesn't it, because they're round the corner, but if you're going on the road?

Lynne: No, if I do it on the road I usually say what hotel I'm in, but I don't ever give the real hotel. Well, I mean, I do give the real hotel, that's a lie, I do give the real hotel, but before I go I find like a janitor closet, like some defunct room, and I give that room number or a floor that doesn't exist.

Author: Have you had problems before with anyone following you home?

Lynne: No. And I have often wondered if I were to be raped or attacked how that would all factor in?

Author: Have you ever upset anyone with that joke?

Lynne: Yeah, many times. Millennials are very sensitive. At the Underground two millennials cried at two separate occasions, and then the Underground told them, "Well, we're not going to ask her to not do the joke, we're really sorry you're sensitive." They're really nice. The Cellar was nice. I mean, like, recently, this is so funny, just a couple of weeks ago some guy had his feet on the stage here at the Cellar, like, balls out, feet on the stage, wearing shorts, it's summer, and I said, "Oh, you're going to keep your feet on the stage? Unbelievable." I said something like that and I made fun of how the people who come to the Comedy Cellar … I say, "I know you people, you're the people who go on safaris, you want to be this close to wild animals, I get it, but you shouldn't … Like, I get that you want to see a rhino up close, but you shouldn't put your feet on the window of the jeep. It's still a rhino. Like, be ready to run." And so as I said that one of the managers here, Val, tapped the guy on the back and he goes, "I just got told to get my feet off the stage." And I go, "Yeah, because they care more about us than you. The animals are more important than the people coming here. Without the animals the zoo doesn't run."

Author: Did he stay for the show?

Lynne: Yeah, he wasn't mad, but so he said to me, "I don't get why they would ask me." Like he was more important.

Author: And with the two women at the Village Underground for the rape joke, how did they complain? Did they come up to you afterwards?

Lynne: Not to me. I was told later. And the club was upset, like, wait staff told me. The club was like, "You shouldn't have been told." Like, they don't want us to change anything, especially that joke.

CHAPTER 149

The Cellar hosts a debate. *Is American Conservativism Hostile to Women?* **The debate is filmed for C-SPAN. The moderator is Kathleen Parker. The panelists are Carol M. Swain, Janus Adams, Sally Kohn and Ann Coulter.**

Author: Leslie Jones was quoted in a *New Yorker* piece, when the reporter was with her in the Cellar and Ann Coulter was there, and Leslie said something like, "What's that frightening bitch doing here?" I don't know if you ever read that?

Noam: I never read that, but you know, they're so much the opposite of me. Like, if I saw someone like Chomsky, or somebody who really stood for everything I disagreed with or really bugged me I'd think, "Awesome, let me go talk to them. I want to have it out with them." I would never be upset that they were there, but it's the common reaction now. They don't relish the idea of talking to them or trying to set them straight or listening to them, whatever it is. I mean, Ann Coulter, she has some views which I certainly won't try to defend. That's not even what it is actually. Her views, I don't think she has any particular view that she can't defend. She's expressed them with a certain flippancy and lack of apparent empathy from time to time in a way that, I understand why people are offended, some of them have offended me, but Ann Coulter is no joke. You read an Ann Coulter book, you are not reading the ramblings of an idiot. And this is what people on both sides of the spectrum do all the time, because it's always easier to dismiss somebody. It's way easier than having to grapple with their arguments.

CHAPTER 148

Author: I interviewed Nick Di Paolo as well, and he was brilliant, really lovely, said nothing but great things, but then he talked about how he hasn't played here for a little while, but because he basically was being rude to the audience.

Estee: No, no, no, it's all his doing. If he calls in his avails I would always book him because he's a really important comic. But yes, he can be brutal. He can be brutal. Oh my god. I would stay in the door downstairs while he was talking and he would use the c-word on a customer and, you know, he says, "Look at the manager, her tits are sweating." But that's Nick Di Paolo on one hand. On the other hand, I can show you ... I will show you text messages, how much he loves me and appreciates me and what I do for them, whatever, on the one hand. On the other hand he says, "Oh look, the manager's tits are sweating."

Author: So he wasn't saying you weren't booking him anymore, he started to feel hostile, he was annoyed ...

Estee: He's always, always on the edge.

Author: And he just felt like he was bringing a negativity, so he sat down with Noam and said, "Look, I'll just stay away for a little bit."

Estee: He's doing shows around the corner.

Author: Is he? Whereabouts?

Estee: At the Fat Black or Village Underground. So he has his own show.

Author: Oh, okay, yeah, okay, when he can properly …

Estee: But not on the line-up, and let me tell you, the truth of the matter is that whenever he was going up I was sweating. Let me tell you. It's scary sometimes.

Author: Noam talked a little bit about that, but he sent me this great email that he sent to a customer about a Sam Morril joke, about the alligator, does that sort of thing happen a lot?

Estee: Well look, when you play to open public, everybody has different sensitivity. I'll tell you a stupid story, okay. There was a comedian that hasn't been here in years. Jeff … He was from Atlanta. Oh my god, he hasn't been here for years. It'll come to me. It'll come to me. And he had a puppet of a raccoon, Rocky Raccoon. And he was working it, you know, and then the joke was, "Oh, I trained my Rocky Raccoon. Rocky, how much is two and two?" And he would take the puppet and smash it on the piano, "Two and two? One, two, three, four." A customer came out crying how cruel he was. I said, "It's a puppet, it's a joke." So you do have different people with different sensitivity and different awareness, with non-awareness of what's going on, you know what I mean? And when something like this happens, what can you do? What can you say? The rape thing, Lynne Koplitz has a rape joke … That'd be an interesting thing, for you to talk to her. She does that rape joke. It's my favorite joke of hers, and nobody is offended. So it all depends how you do it. And then, if you have a rape victim in and you're crass about it, then yeah, they're going to be upset, and yes, look, there's one thing, we do not tell people, comics, what to talk about or what's forbidden. There's no censorship whatsoever. I have the option not to book you if I feel that you are alienating more than you are entertaining. You are in the business of entertainment. You want to get on a soapbox? Go ahead, open a new speakeasy or something, leave my stage alone. So it's important that the comics are intelligent. That's what I think most comics are, super-intelligent, quick on their feet, interesting, but if you make a comment about something and people get offended? It's on them, not on the comic. If you come out of the gate to offend people? Then no, I don't like it, but that makes sense, doesn't it?

Author: Well, I think it's about intent, and if you get it wrong then you get it wrong, and there's stuff that I hear a comic say, like it might be about an illness in your family or something like that, and all it does is make me … I don't laugh at it, but I wouldn't go and complain about it, because everyone's got their thing.

Estee: Yeah, but you see, the art of stand-up comedy is unique in this matter, as opposed to any other art form, if you are a singer and somebody writes your words, if you're an actor, somebody writes your script. They are naked on that stage and it's them and their perspective. As I said, most of them, they're above average intelligence, above average, and so if somebody complains, sometimes it's valid, sometimes it's not. Sometimes it's not valid. So I just don't say anything. If it's valid I acknowledge it: sorry.

CHAPTER 147

The author asks Sam Morril if he can quote from Sam's email. The bit the author wants to quote is when Sam says it's a terrible time to be a comedian. Sam says sure, but he's worried about coming off badly in the book. He says being taken out of context is scary. The author understands. A book is different from a room.

CHAPTER 146

Erika: Who makes a joke about a child who just died? But what I was thinking the whole time was, what if I had been his mother? I guess if I were his mother I probably wouldn't be at a comedy club right after my child died. But even, like, years later, you know, just as a mother of a son or any child for that matter, but I have a little boy, I just felt like I should leave. Just to, like, be respectful to her, you know? Even if the rest of his show was fine, I just was so disgusted. And I'm not a very emotional person. I actually hardly ever cry. It's kind of a joke. Like, "Why do you not cry when you're a girl?" But I cried.

Author: Did you really?

Erika: I was just so upset. That story.

Author: Where did you cry?

Erika: Like, walking out of the club, and I stopped and talked to ... I don't know if it was the manager. I think it was the manager. I talked to a few people and they were kind of rude too. They basically said, and I hate to summarize as it's been a long time, "If you don't like what he's saying then you don't have to stay." It wasn't like, "We're sorry, we didn't know that he was going to say that joke ahead of time," or, "We would have said no." I don't know if they do that but ...

Author: No, I think they don't, they wouldn't stop anybody from saying anything. But I guess there's always a point at which they might say ...

Erika: Ah, okay.

Author: I guess they'd just stop booking a comedian if they didn't like what they said.

Erika: That's true.

Author: So some people would watch it and say it was an overreaction. This is why I'm asking you. Like, had you had a lot to drink? Had you had one cocktail? Or two cocktails or something?

Erika: No, I don't think it was from drinking. I mean, it wasn't like I was hysterical. I was just like, "Oh my god, I cannot believe someone wrote a joke about this child." It wasn't like I was hysterical. I just had, like, tears in my eyes and I told my husband. I was even frustrated that he didn't immediately stand up to leave too. I was like, "What are you doing? I'm not listening to this guy." And he was like, "Oh, okay." He was really ... He thought it was bad but not as bad as me I guess.

Author: He wasn't laughing?

Erika: No, not at all.

Author: He sat at the table and ...

Erika: He was just like, "Wow," and then as we talked about it the more he thought about it, the more he thought it was horrible too, but he was like, "I'm proud of you for taking this stance." Not that it really matters, I'm one person, but I was just like, gosh, this person, if nothing else he should just maybe think a little more about talking about children. I just feel like children are off limits. Everything else you can joke about I guess.

CHAPTER 145

Before that, Erika receives an email from the Comedy Cellar,

Thank you for coming to the Comedy Cellar. We are always trying to improve, and we find that honest customer feedback is the most valuable resource we have. If you have a chance, please let us know what you enjoyed and what you thought could have been better. We cannot promise a reply to each and every email, however we do answer quite a few every week. Every email comment we receive is read carefully by the owners. Please be blunt.

Erika replies,

Okay you want blunt, I'll be blunt. I had the worst comedy experience of my life at your venue last night. A disgusting person, I won't call him a comedian because he's not humorous, Sam Morril, took the stage and spent the first few minutes of his act disrespecting Lane Graves, the two-year-old child who was murdered by the alligator at Disney. He even cracked "jokes" about his parents and his funeral. I have never in my life been so offended and repulsed by someone. I immediately left and stopped to tell your staff why. They followed me to make sure my drinks were being paid not because I had just had to listen to a sick man try to use a child's death as a pathetic shock value attempt at being a comedian.

Furthermore, upon speaking with friends who worked for a comedy club for over ten years, I learned that your venue had to know his set prior to him taking the stage which meant someone approved of this garbage. You should be ashamed of yourselves too. The girl who was introducing all the acts simply replied to my outrage with "different people are offended by different things." Oh really?! I would expect all human beings would be offended by a sicko making jokes about a 2-year-old baby's tragic death, saying his mother probably said "later gator" at his funeral, etc. I have posted about this on every social media account I own and asked people to share it. The comedian himself replied to me to say "pretty strong act huh? Tonight was my first time trying that one out." What a complete and utter pathetic excuse for a human. He doesn't deserve to breathe the same air or live on the same planet as that precious little boy's family. So there's my review. The other acts were fine. I really enjoyed the staff girl who introduced everyone until I received her heartless rude response to my feedback. She can fly a kite too.

Noam asks Liz if anything was left out. Liz says not. Noam replies,

I'm a parent with two small children and I completely understand your reaction to Sam's joke. Comedians generally hold nothing sacred. For them, the bizarre nature of the incident inspires a kind of gallows humor which others may find offensive or just not funny. To be very clear, no, we don't approve of any comedians' material before they take the stage. You note in your email that this was the first time that he told the joke, so not only did we not approve it, we had no way of knowing he was going to say it, since he had never said it before. But even if we had known what he was going to say, I have to tell you that I would not have intervened. I cannot censor the artists who appear at my venue. Believe me, sometimes I would like to but I can't. You simply can't imagine the resentment that I would engender if I were to tell Louis CK, who has done jokes about pedophilia that were controversial, or any other comedian, what they can or can't say. Stand-up comedy by nature lives close to the line. What one person considers thought-provoking another considers irreverently funny and another considers unacceptably offensive. It's simply impossible to lay down an objective standard that everyone could agree on. It's the same reason the First Amendment is interpreted so broadly. It's virtually impossible to decide what speech is acceptable and what can be forbidden. In the end it would all become about not offending me and my particular sensibilities. As a club owner, all I can do is stop booking a comedian if they are not doing well with the audience, and that determination can't be made after any one set that did or did not go well. All the comedians have bad sets and almost all offend someone at some time in their careers. Having said all that, it's no pleasure for me that you left unhappy. If there's anything I can do, perhaps refund your cover charges or invite you back to a better show as my guest, please just say the word. I hope this has been helpful to you in some way.

CHAPTER 144

Days earlier, Erika's on holiday with her husband. It's their first time away since becoming parents. They love comedy. The Cellar has great reviews, plus it's in a fun part of town. They get tickets. Liza Treyger is the emcee. She does her Holocaust jizz joke. She usually does her Holocaust jizz joke if a darker comedian's coming on, just to get it out of the crowd's system. Liza introduces Sam. He asks if anyone heard about the baby who was killed by an alligator. He doesn't use the child's name. He says baby instead of child. He says he doesn't want to come across as a right-wing nut, but maybe if the baby was carrying a gun? He asks if anyone watched the televised funeral. It wasn't televised, that's part of the joke. He describes what he saw. Erika stands up and walks out of the showroom. On her way out she complains to Liza. Liza tells her people are offended by different things and she can leave if she wants. She leaves. She cries. She tweets,

Comic @sammorril makes part of act jokes about 2 yr old being killed by alligator in Disney. He should be boycotted. I left immediately

Sam retweets it and adds his comment. Other people tweet to Erika. Sam doesn't want it to be a thing. He feels bad. Erika reads the tweets from strangers,

People like you don't belong at comedy shows

It's called a comedy show, they tell jokes and shouldn't be politically correct.

Comedians should have most freedom of speech

So his set was fine until he made a joke YOU were sensitive about?

if something offends you then it has too much power over you (Louie CK)

I hope your baby is eaten by an alligator, and then gets reincarnated into an alligator and eats your 2nd baby

CHAPTER 143

An alligator kills Lane Graves.

CHAPTER 142

The author phones Noam about the book proposal he's writing,

Author: I think I said in the email that it's like an empire, and you've taken over this empire, and someone I was talking to, I think my agent, said it's like an allegory for America, you know, this great empire, booming, expanding, but somewhere on the horizon, everyone's wondering, when is this boom going to end? When is the downturn coming? I wondered how much that's in your thoughts?

Noam: All the time. It's all the time in my thoughts. I was just talking to Dan Naturman about this. You know, I try to fairly assess what my contribution has been without arrogantly assessing it. So, for instance, comedy is booming now, the Comedy Cellar is booming now, and some of that can be luck. On the other hand, the other comedy clubs are not booming, so clearly it wasn't pre-ordained that it would have to be booming now, as opposed to and distinct from the previous years of boom, where every comedy club was booming and they could just open up and people would pour in. It's not that kind of boom right now. Right now the Comedy Cellar is, I think, quite often attracting eighty or ninety per cent of all the people in Manhattan who are going out to see comedy on any given night. So that means we've done certain things very well and I think there's a certain kind of … One really good comedy club makes it hard to have any other good comedy clubs, because there's not that many good comedians. There's really like fifteen, twenty really good comedians in town on any given night, if that many. And I mean, even if you compare it to a baseball team, you have the nine best players in the country or something on your line-up, but even in that line-up, the end of the line-up is still batting two hundred. So even among the best of the best there's a huge difference. Even among the best of the best comedians, if twenty of them are in town, really only about seven or eight of them are home-run hitters. So, as I have opened up so many shows and have so much space and am giving all these best comics three or four spots in a night, they are not playing anywhere else. And that's, I think, made it very hard for the other clubs. And then social media. Everybody's very well informed these days. So they're aware of it. Years ago they wouldn't have known that. So that's helped me. On the other hand, there's no place to go but down, which scares me, and eventually it will go down, you know.

The author asks if Noam's children will take over one day,

Noam: Well, I hope so. You know, it's funny. I even put it on Facebook, my daughter said something so funny to me yesterday. She said something, and I wasn't paying attention I guess, or I didn't laugh, and she said, "Daddy, is that funny?" And I'm like, "Yeah, that's funny." And she goes, "Well, you didn't laugh." I said, "I know, I'm sorry." She said, "Listen, Daddy, if you laugh I know it's funny, if you don't laugh I don't know if you didn't think it was funny or it's not funny at all." This was my four-year-old daughter. And I said, "That's all you need to know to run comedy shows. If they don't laugh, it's not funny or they didn't think it was funny, and that's it." So, I mean, that's not an answer. I don't know how long it will last. I own the building where the Olive Tree is, and I don't own the Underground, so I guess if it deteriorated, the first thing I could do is close the Underground and just the run the Comedy Cellar as it was originally. I said something to my wife recently. I said, "Listen, if it ever gets back to the point where we're struggling to make ends meet, I think I just want to sell it or get out, but I don't want to live that way again." My father had and I have a little PTSD from the years when things were very tough.

CHAPTER 141

Author: When did you kind of decide to stop telling that joke?

Gregg Rogell: Well, after watching the special I didn't like it. I didn't like it. Personally, whenever I watch anything I've done I don't like it, I'm very critical of it, so I tend to, once I put it out there, I stop doing it in general. But since being to the Middle East I really regret it. I think a lot of people, it would benefit them if they saw more of the world. You tend to, before I traveled ... I mean I've traveled abroad during my career. I've been to England, Amsterdam, but until I supported Russell Peters ... With Russell Peters I was in Africa, I was in Kenya, I was all over India, Sri Lanka, I've been to these places and you meet these people and, you know, Americans, we seem to think that anywhere out of America is kind of Third World, and it's not. Some of the places we stayed, especially like the hotels, they blow America away. Some of these hotels in India and the Middle East, China, the toilets, they clean your ass for you. We don't even have that here. It really gives you perspective, you know? So now I'm very careful with my material as far as, I don't like really making fun of other cultures. I make fun of myself.

CHAPTER 140

Gregg: Three weeks before the tour we got a call. I got a call from Russell's brother that the promoter in Jordan said that I couldn't go on because I'm Jewish and he was concerned, because he has to work there, and there's going to be a lot of Palestinians in the audience and it could be a controversial thing, so I can't go on, but I'm welcome to go to Jordan you know.

Author: That's really shocking, that because you're Jewish, no matter where in the world for me, you shouldn't be stopped from going on a stage.

Gregg: If they can let me go on in Saudi Arabia, why can't they let me go on in Jordan? But as it turned out, I did go on in Jordan. The day of the show, during the sound check, Russell's brother had them shine my name on the back of the stage, and the promoter said, "He's not going on," and then Russell's brother, Clayton, said, "Yeah, he is going on." Clayton put his foot down and said, "He's going on." So I went on and I killed. They loved me. And then Russell came on and he said, "How about a hand for Gregg Rogell?" And he kind of whispered, "He's a Jew." And again, they all laughed. There was a big laugh. But nobody cared. It was not an issue at all.

CHAPTER 139

Gregg: No, I didn't talk about any religion in those countries. You avoid it, religion, politics and explicit sexual material but, you know, you can curse.

CHAPTER 138

The Cellar hosts its first debate. The subject is the Iran deal. The panelists are Alan Dershowitz, Fred Kaplan, Matthew Kroenig and Jim Walsh.

Author: I wondered if you could put into words why you value people being able to openly debate, to debate honestly?

Noam: I just find it interesting. I don't know how to put it. I just … It's just part of my nature to, you know, think about things and the first question I have is, "What am I missing? What are the arguments on the other side?" And then sometimes you really don't know whether … Nothing is as convincing as seeing someone who can't defend their position. In other words, people say, "Blah, blah, blah," but when you see someone in a debate and you realize they haven't got an answer to that, and somebody asks another question, they haven't got an answer to that. That is the most effective way to change somebody's mind and the most effective way to demonstrate that a position is weak. What we have now, most of the time, is just somebody making arguments and they very, very rarely, more than ever, they very, very rarely present the opposing arguments in their best light. So what you read mostly, even in the best newspapers now, is a takedown of a diluted, unfair version of the other side, and then they declare victory and move on. And, you know, it's just not interesting to me.

CHAPTER 137

Jordan Sargent writes a story about Louis CK for *Gawker*. The weekend after it's published he's in his apartment reading the responses. There's an email from a name he knows.

Jordan: If you wanted to include this in whatever you're writing you could say it's some sort of well-known Hollywood person. You can anonymize it in some way. I don't want her name to be in the story. Anyway, we can go back on the record.

Author: So her name's off the record?

Jordan: Yeah. Just not her name. You can anonymize it in some way. So she emailed me and was like, oh, I forget exactly what she said, but like, "I've heard all this kind of stuff about Louis before, let me try and like gather some stories for you." And she emailed this duo. She emailed them and she was like, "I really think ... You guys, this reporter's trying to write about Louis CK, I really think you should talk to him." And they responded to her and she forwarded me the email and they said, "We don't want to talk about this. If we talk about this no one will ever book us again."

CHAPTER 136

Author: You had a big argument with Noam where you were saying ... This is maybe two or three years ago, downstairs, where you were saying ... He was talking about club owners on the road and how you had to give them a bit more slack ... You were kind of having a go at club owners. And you said, "This is nothing to do with you, you didn't build this place," or something like that?

Robert Kelly: I did?

Author: Yeah.

Robert: When?

Author: Two or three years ago.

Robert: Where'd you get this?

Author: From Noam.

Robert: I said that?

Author: Do you remember having a big argument with him downstairs?

Robert: No. I mean, I think ... It's weird that you say that because

... I hope he's quoting the right thing. I think Noam has a big part of this.

Author: "This is nothing to do with you"?

Robert: What?

Author: I guess the Cellar?

Robert: Oh no, that's crazy.

Author: I don't think he thinks you meant it, but you got angry at the time.

Robert: I don't think ... I don't remember saying that. I really don't. I just know that his father ... His father ... It was weird, because his father so loved this place. Estee, Ava and his father were this place. And they just really cultivated their own breed of comic, almost like a team. Like a league or something. And they made you feel like you had a home and they took care of you. It was just this surrogate family that they created for all of us. They had a big part of us becoming a community you know.

Author: A lot of people have told me Manny was like a dad to them.

Robert: I loved Manny, because one time I said, "You're like my family." He goes, "Look, this is business."

Author: Did he say that?

Robert: He goes, "This is business."

Author: How did you react to that?

Robert: I remember one time Manny actually said, "You can't work the other clubs."

Author: Specifically the Boston round the corner wasn't it? Where did he say that?

Robert: Right downstairs. He took me from the table to another table. He says, "I've got to talk to you." He goes, "You can't work the Boston. I can't have people working here and then working there." And I said, "Well, that sucks Manny that you say that, because I really care about you and I love you guys and I consider you like my family." He goes, "This isn't family, this is business." And I was like, "Okay, that's what you think, but I'm going to have to say, I have bills and things to pay, and that's business, and I really don't want to not work here, but I can't have you tell me where I can and can't work. That's crazy." And he went, "Alright, you can work the club."

CHAPTER 135

Noam: With Robert Kelly, we had one fight at the table where he was talking about how road clubs are ... Clubs on the road can be very ... "They pay badly and blah blah blah and they don't ..." And I was trying to tell him that I thought they're probably not being as greedy as you think they are because they struggle. And for people who can't draw on their name, which is a lot of comedians, the people go to the comedy club and they see somebody they've never heard of. And people who can't draw on their name, they don't have the right to be demanding anything top-dollar because they're not the reason that the people are in the club. Anyway, I was trying to explain to him the business aspect of it and he lost his shit, screaming and yelling at me.

Author: Because he thought you were implying he's not a draw?

Noam: No. I can see why ... From the way I said it ... That wasn't it, because he is a draw, you know.

Author: Was it because you were trying to tell him about the business?

Noam: He just didn't want to hear the other side of the story. This is not unique to comedians. This is anybody on the receiving end of any power structure, they always want to believe that the other side is just, you know, the most ... And the people on their side, "We're the good ones." And it's never the case. It's like, I don't know if you've had this experience, but I've had it. People hate landlords. They hate landlords until they invest in a condo or become a landlord in any way, in which case they're like, "Holy shit, this is ridiculous. These tenants don't have to pay their rent." They're literally shocked. Dumbfounded. There's that famous George McGovern column in the *Wall Street Journal*, you should look it up. You know who George McGovern is, don't you?

Author: Yeah, yeah.

Noam: And after a whole career in the Senate, basically the most liberal Senator in the country, he left the Senate to open a small bed-and-breakfast-type place. And a year and a half later he went bankrupt and he wrote a column about his experience, essentially saying, and I think I'm being fair to him, saying that, "If I had known then what I know now, I just wouldn't have voted the way I voted."

CHAPTER 134

Artic Lange does a spot at the Cellar. He tells a joke about being fat and having sex with someone. @cherrell_brown watches then tweets,

Almost got kicked out of Olive Tree Cafe bar down in the Village ...

So there a comedy show downstairs where the bathroom is, and I have to walk by the comedian/stage to go to the bathroom

There's this white guy who starts a joke with "... these protests are messing with my personal ..." so I stop to listen ...

"I was having sex w/this black chick, & she said 'I can't breathe' and I said 'come on don't bring politics into the bedroom.'"

The majority white audience cackled and laughed. I flung my braids over my shoulder, pointed at a group and said "that shit ain't funny"

Then got escorted back upstairs

A black person's dying words become punch lines.

They looked at me perplexed as to why I was angry. I mean the entire room was doubled over in laughter, yall.

I'm still here and I'm going to get the comedians name.

They walked my ass back upstairs and now have someone at the door.

Got a name ...

So comedian @artiequitter thinks it's funny to make #ICantBreathe jokes at the expense of Eric Garner at @NYCComedyCellar tonight

Dear @NYCComedyCellar don't book bigots like @artiequitter again. I will be sharing his offensive and disgusting routine w/folks

Wow, clearly @artiequitter has a reputation already. Def didn't know dude before tonight. You're an awfully unfunny bigot.

If @NYCComedyCellar supports acts like @artiequitter then we don't need to support their business!!

Here's the painful kicker, everyone laughed yall. I almost cried.

If yall don't get out my mentions with "it's comedy," "what do you expect from him?" "move on" type responses. Bye

We have to let establishments like @NYCComedyCellar know we're not accepting this racist shit. Not even in the name of comedy

I also found out from a server that @artiequitter is a regular at @NYCComedyCellar. Think yall should end that agreement

Or I will find out the next time he is performing and come disrupt his disrespect, racist, act

And you'll say "but jokes. But comedy." But if we were talking the holo-caust or the Boston marathon you'd be outraged. #BlackLivesMatter too

@NYCComedyCellar if you don't cancel @artiequitter were bringing the protest to you

This isn't just a/b police accountability. Never was. This is about valuing black lives & disrupting anything that perpetuates the opposite yall. I was suppose to be here with Emerald, Eric Garner's daughter, tonight having a bday drink. She got sick. What if she came & heard that?

He managed to make a violent joke about BW and mock Black Death. @artiequitter is trash

Now @artiequitter is RTing me. Keep it cute, until we show up to protest at your shows. We got dates, homie.

Now his fans are all up and through my mentions with rape threats

Rape threats. Bitch. Cunt. Humorless whore. Die. All in the last 20 mins. White supremacy defending itself, folks

CHAPTER 133

Author: So that was your second album? Wow. And I wondered if there was any backlash on that? Because a lot of what I'm trying to write is showing how, you know, audiences change, and public discourse, and people being offended, and how they react to how they feel about jokes and stuff like that. And because you're one of the ... A lot of the Cellar people are quite over towards the Conservative side. And you're quite on the Liberal side. And I wondered if people ever reacted badly to you using that word on the stage?

Ted Alexandro: No, I never got any pushback. It definitely, like, when you say that word on stage, you know, you can feel the energy in the room change. They're listening very ... They're kind of on high alert. But I think the fact that I use it as a quote, like the girl that I was dating who was black used the word, so to me then it was just a matter ... Like, I would never use the word myself, just saying it on stage, but I had to kind of weigh the value and import of, "Do I use the word and does it benefit the joke?" And I think ultimately I felt like I had to use the word because it just heightens the circumstances of the joke, and I'm quoting her so, yeah, but never any blowback.

CHAPTER 132

Author: So when you were trying to figure that out, did you try doing it on stage saying "n-word"?

Ted: I don't know that I ever said "n-word." Yeah, no, I think … I'll tell you this, it was a bit that I shelved for a while. I put it away because I couldn't figure out how to do it properly in a way that to me felt justified that it landed where it needed to land comedically and, you know, as far as telling a story. But then once I finally got the ending of, "it was like my own civil war, north against south, brother against brother," like because I say how I froze, like, "When she said it I froze from the waist up, but I kept fucking her, so it was the most racist ejaculation I ever had. It was like my own civil war, brother against brother, north against south, except this time the south won." So yeah, when I got all of the pieces to it finally I felt like, yes, I need to say the n-word in the joke because it was such a visceral thing that really happened in my life. So sometimes, for me, you work backwards from something real that happened, you know, that wasn't necessarily funny in the moment but it was visceral.

Author: She really did say that?

Ted: Yes, that was true. I wouldn't make something like that up, you know. Like, yeah, that really happened, so yeah, then it was just a matter of like, how do I tell it in a way that's true for me, and if it offends anyone I'll be okay with it. You know.

[After one hour and seventeen minutes]

Ted: Anytime you're talking about something of that nature, specifically the n-word, which is in its own category for me, I feel like you'd better have comedic and personal justification for why you're using it. So … Especially as a white comic. So for me I had to … And like I said, I shelved that joke for months and months but then came back around to it and figured it out.

Author: Do you remember when you had that experience? What year?

Ted: You know, I remember that it was around the time that I was opening for Louis, because I remember that he talked to me about the joke one time, and kind of helped me with the breakthrough in the sense that when I first did it I was telling it and trying to find more of a jokey ending, and then he said, like, "Well what really happened?" And I said, "Well I just … I kept fucking her." And he's like, you know, "Try that."

CHAPTER 131

Rachel Feinstein: This other thing happened, I don't know if this fits in with anything, but it gives you an idea of what it was like on the road. I flew across country. I got to the casino. It's this long awful week. It's, like, Tuesday through Saturday, you know? Comics hate that long Vegas weekend. It's just so lonely and isolating. And so I get there Tuesday and my room key isn't working. I walk back down, all the way down, bring my luggage up and down. They give me another key and then I walk back up again and it's not working, that second key, so then I walk back down again I was like, "My key's not working." And then they said … It turns out it was like the magnetic thing on the door, you know, and there wasn't an extra room, so they sent the mechanic up to fix it. So I was sitting in the hallway of the hotel while the mechanic was fixing it, and he's chatting with me. He was really nice and he was like, "Oh, that must be lonely, just like being this woman on the road." And I was like, "Yeah, it's hard," and whatever. We talked a little bit. He was really overly friendly to me. And then he leaves. Then the next night my boyfriend at the time came to visit me and at four in the morning this mechanic walked into my room. Like, open the door, walked into my room, standing over the bed, you know.

Author: Your boyfriend was there?

Rachel: Yeah, but think if he wasn't. I would have been assaulted. So I got up. I screamed. He got up and grabbed the guy, pushed him out of the room. The guy ran down the hallway. So we called downstairs and the mechanic tried to claim that he thought there was a call from my room. First of all, even if there was a call, why would you walk into the place, you know? And then I tried to call everybody and, like, try to get them to take this seriously, because I don't want this guy to do this to somebody else.

Author: Yeah, it's really psychopathic.

Rachel: Finally, one person at the casino was like, "Yeah, well maybe he didn't ... maybe he ..." I said, "I want to know the calls. I want to know all the calls he had that night because there's got to be a record of which room." And so he finally told me, and when I was like hassling them they just wanted me to shut up about it, give me like a nicer room, and then he's like, "Well, you're right, the last call was in a different tower, hours before, on a different floor. So there's no way that he was called to your room." And he said, "We're going to look into this." And I told everybody that would listen, but it's like ... But they all just kind of quietened it. But it just shows how vulnerable you are. If my boyfriend hadn't been there I don't know what would have happened to me that night. I really don't.

CHAPTER 130

Kurt Metzger: He called the cops to say I assaulted him, but the crowd, luckily, was like, "No, he attacked the comic." He was trying to show off because his girl's like a model or something. And on stage what I do when somebody sucks is I let them annoy the crowd before I make fun of ... The rookie mistake is to try and do ... Or what I would do wrong when I was new was, I would go mean too hard too fast on somebody, but now what I do is let the audience ... Because sometimes the audience has no idea how bad someone's fucking you up by talking. So I wait until I can see that they're, "Are you going to do something about this person?" Because you need like a mandate from them, you know. Once you have that, you can do whatever you want, but I still didn't make it that confrontational. I was, like, you know, I go, "Does this girl get you in a lot of fights man?" I was trying to give him ways out, but he was drunk and I think that he felt his wife was too hot for him so he had to show off.

Author: And I just want to go back to the start of it, I think you were on a podcast talking about it. I think that you said the woman shouted, "You suck"?

Kurt: Yeah, it was weird, because it wasn't like I was bombing. I was doing well with the crowd. So I ignored it for a minute.

Author: So you ignored it, told another joke and people laughed and then ...

Kurt: And then I go, "Maybe it's you who sucks?" I don't know. I said something. It's not an overly … And then I said, I mean, this is kind of a stock line that I use, but I told her that she's very attractive, "And that's probably why you think that people want you to talk a lot, but you know, that's a lie they tell you because you're pretty." I said it, not even that … You need to go through a comeback line. And then this guy goes, "I'll fucking kick your ass." But I still wasn't … I mean, I wasn't taking it seriously that there was going to be a fight. I was thirty-six or thirty-seven. I was a little old to be getting in a fist fight.

Author: That's when you said, "Seriously, does this girl get you in fights a lot?"

Kurt: Yeah and he goes, "That's fine, I win fights." He really was aggressive. I just had to … I didn't want to ruin my set, you know, so when I got off stage, that's when I kind of fucked up, because I was just dying to know who this was wanting to fight me. Jay had kind of defused it. Even he was kind of making fun of me, because I had this long coat on. I can't remember what he was calling me.

Author: What did he say?

Kurt: He called me the Equalizer or some shit. It was fine, there was no need for it to be a fight, but I guess this is where … I wouldn't do this again if I had to go back, because I wouldn't have got my eardrum popped, but I looked over and this girl was, like, stunning. She must have been like some kind of hot shit in Texas. That's where they were from, Texas. And I go, "Oh, hey, Jay, I was right she's like a hot bitch." I said it like in an urban sense of the word. Whatever. I said it slang. She goes, "Don't call me a bitch." And I lost my temper then, because I mean, she was a huge bitch. So I go, "Oh no sweetie, I'm calling him a bitch and I'm calling you a cunt." But I was in the door, I wasn't on the stage. So when I said that the dude got up. And

I still didn't understand that he was going to hit me. And I had my neck all the way out. And I remember I was going, hey, he's coming over here. Like, no guard or nothing. And he just cupped his hand. I didn't even see it happen. I just felt pop.

CHAPTER 129

Author: Whose side did you take?

Noam: I took my side. I mean, I didn't take anybody's side. I took the side of … Look, I mean, Kurt called the guy's wife a cunt. Now that's never a good idea. It's fighting words, and of course the guy hit him. You're never supposed to hit somebody just because they call your wife a cunt, but it's a predictable outcome when you do call somebody's wife a cunt. So I thought Kurt shouldn't have called her a cunt. I thought the guy should not have hit Kurt. I thought Kurt shouldn't have hit him back. It's a whole unfortunate sequence of events, but in the end if there was anybody who was really legally wrong it was the guy who took the first swing, which was the audience member.

Author: So this is like, you're dealing with a business where strange things happen, because if you ran a doughnut shop those things wouldn't be happening, but you're dealing with people who've had alcohol, and you're dealing with comedians who are sometimes difficult …

Noam: And you know, the thing is, I have no control over what they do on stage, and the first person who's going to get a lawsuit is me.

CHAPTER 128

Author: If you're going to own a business, a major motivation is money, and it's a motivation for all of us in our jobs and stuff. But why would you pay more money than other clubs? Is it just because it benefits the business in the long run?

Noam: Well, first of all there's two things I'm thinking about. First of all, as far as money goes, they say a black hole has such a gravitational force it actually bends light and time. Money seems to have that effect on people's reasoning. It is such a powerful motivator that they will rationalize the most ridiculous distortions of logic and truth to work backwards into the situation where they maximise their money. I have seen it over and over and over again, where people, out of their mouths will come things where if they were listening to it from a third party they would just laugh. But not only do they say it, they believe it. This is the powerful effect of money. I'm sure the Bible has similar observations on it. So it's really true. And the next question is, why would you pay people more? Well, yeah, there's two reasons. One reason is that it's better for the business to pay people more because the more you pay the more everybody gives you their first choice of spots, and the more everybody feels good about the place, and the more everybody wants to be there and puts on their A-game and is afraid of tossing their sets. And, you know, for a million reasons everybody respects the place that they have the best feeling about the most. And then also, when business is good you feel guilty, but this is more than with the comedians, it's the people who aren't comedians who work much harder for less money at the Cellar.

CHAPTER 127

Noam has opened a second comedy room, the Village Underground, on Third Street. It used to be his live music venue. He's decorated it the same as the Cellar. It seats about two-hundred. It's a short walk from the Comedy Cellar.

Author: There must have been a lot of eyebrows raised when that opened at first?

Noam: Yeah, there were, but my father would have been all for it, no question he would have been all for it. There's no way we were going to be turning away the number of people we were turning away. Here's the thing, many people's instinct at that point would have been to raise the prices. That instinctually goes against my philosophy and his philosophy. You don't want to raise prices because you don't want to do anything to bring down demand. Essentially when you raise the prices you always lose customers. Now it's true, if you have overflow you may not feel it, but at some point as business dips, all of a sudden you're going to have empty seats, so expanding was a way better way to go than raising prices. As a matter of fact, I was able to lower some prices by expanding. He would have been all for that.

CHAPTER 126

Author: The Stand opened in 2012. Greenwich Village Comedy Club opened up in 2012. You opened the Village Underground for comedy in 2013 and it seemed like ... I know you had big lines so wanted to ensure you made use of that business, but was it also to increase capacity of shows so comedians didn't have to play anywhere else? Was it a way of muscling out the Stand?

Noam: No. No. No. No, not at all, not even a little bit. It was always simply that we were turning away ... The first thing I did was rewrite the website, and this part I did actually to give me a count of exactly how many people we were turning away from each show. And when I saw the numbers, literally like a thousand people on a Saturday night were being turned away, I decided to do it. I mean, I wasn't motivated by the effect on the other clubs. As a matter of fact I always caution people in my organization that it's not good for us if other clubs go out of business.

CHAPTER 125

Nick Di Paolo: I didn't even put up a fight. I didn't. Because I know I had a few incidents, a string of incidents. I didn't even argue. I said to Noam, "You and your dad have been nothing but great to me. This club's been nothing but great to me." I remember saying to Noam, "I even remember nights leaving here when I felt bad about what I did." I gave no resistance, because I had no argument. He didn't say, "You can't come back to the club," or anything. But that was a demarcation point, because I sort of suspended myself from the club. I really respect the place so much, and Estee and everybody who runs it. I really didn't want to disrespect it. So I started coming down a little less and little less and it wasn't because I was mad at them. I just wanted to show them the respect they deserve. But I put up no resistance. I agreed with him one hundred per cent. I really like those people a lot.

Author: And do you remember what the incident was that kind of brought that discussion about?

Nick: No. It was a string of them.

Author: So basically, you'd been getting a bit grumpy on stage with the audience?

Nick: I'm always cantankerous, even when I started. It's just my nature. One night I do remember a table of, like, NYU students, young girls. Some girl going, "You're just being racist." I hadn't even really said anything yet and I just fucking went off on her and I said, "Why don't you go and jump off the fucking library?" Because a couple of students had committed suicide, like, three of them within a year had jumped off the library roof. And so I said, "Why don't you go fucking scale the side of that library at NYU?" You know. I don't even remember. It's just a tirade. I just remember them leaving and like some of the girls crying and then ... That's not the first time. I'd look in the doorway and there'd be like seven comics who came downstairs because somebody went up and said, "Nick's on one of his tirades." And that's how many times it would happen. So that's why I didn't give Noam any resistance when he brought it up. But yeah, I'd go fucking nuts. Someone just not paying attention or giving me, like, a dirty look, and I remember, like, knocking their hat off. And I remember even the bouncer goes, "Nick, what the fuck are you doing?" I just got way too comfortable there, you know what I mean? And it was ridiculous. And I knew it. I knew it was time to go and find another club.

CHAPTER 124

Nick: I would talk to Colin at night on the phone, we still do almost all the time, about flying off the handle. And you know, always the word "cunt" would come into play. Again, if I was in England nobody would blink, you know. But you know, the business we're in, comedians, we're such cut-throats. Nobody would say shit except for Colin. Colin is the exception, but you know the rest of the comics, if they think it's going to help them move up a notch in the Comedy Cellar line-up they'll watch you light yourself on fire every night.

Author: And what did Colin say to you?

Nick: He just said, you know, he goes, "You're angry, you're fucking … You get too angry, and calling women cunts every other week or whatever." And literally he goes, "I'm just afraid in the long run it'll come back to bite you in the ass."

Author: And did he mean with the club or with …

Nick: No, he meant in general. You know, because it's funny. I don't associate comedy clubs with real show business, but there is a link there. People do come down to the Comedy Cellar and who knows who's in the audience that night. I remember coming offstage when I called Hillary Clinton a cunt and Jerry Seinfeld was standing in the doorway. He wasn't standing where I could see him. I come through the doorway and he looks at me and goes, "Cunt, huh? Brilliant." And I go, "Hey, I've been here too long." He goes, "You're telling me."

CHAPTER 123

Author: Does he still come here now?

Noam: Yeah.

Author: Okay, because there was that thing where he thought he got the light.

Noam: Wow. No, that was diffused pretty quickly.

Author: Yeah? How?

Noam: Tom Papa called him and he said, "Alright Tom, we can solve this pretty quickly. I'll tell you where the light is and you tell me if I'm wrong." And he said, "When you're on the stage the light is to your left." And Tom said, "No, no, the light's by the door." So Jerry said, "Oh, I guess it wasn't the light." And that was it.

Steve Fabricant: Why would Jerry get off anyway if he got the light?

Noam: He was insulted. I understand that. Not only did he get off, he said, "I'll never be back here again." That's what he said.

Author: But he's been back?

Noam: Yeah.

Ava Har'el: The best comedians pay attention to the light.

Noam: No, but we don't give Seinfeld the light. It was probably the way the gels are on the lighting fixtures. If they don't cut them just right, from a particular angle the white shines through.

Ava: Or maybe somebody took a picture?

Noam: No, I don't think it was that.

Steve: Good guess though.

Noam: No, no, I think it's what I said, because I know from being on stage and it can look like the light.

Author: I thought maybe someone had given him the light, like another comedian or something, just as, like, a prank or something like that.

Noam: No, no, there was no light. Everybody's scared of Seinfeld.

CHAPTER 122

Tom Papa: I remember thinking it's not a big deal. Like, "Noam and Estee are probably worrying too much about this." But then when he was so specific about where the light was, I was like, "Oh, maybe it does bother him?" But it was in a totally different spot. He always loved that place and he loved it especially those years when he would come and sit with Colin and the other comics. It was a cool spot for him, but honestly, the only reason that he'll sometimes go to Gotham Comedy Club more than the Comedy Cellar is that he can park right in front of the place. That's literally what it is. They put out two parking cones, he pulls up on Twenty-Third Street, a guy sits there and watches his car, he walks in and does a spot, and gets in his car and leaves. To go to the Village, they don't care whose car it is, it can't stay out front. If you park on the side it's a problem. If he parks in the garage, now he has to wait two minutes. That's not going to work for him. That's literally all it comes down to.

CHAPTER 121

Dan Soder: I got off stage and Noam was standing there and he was like, "Dan Soder, Dave Chappelle." And he was standing with Dave Chappelle and I was like, "Hey man, nice to meet you." He's like, "Hey, nice to meet you." He said something like … I don't want to quote him because I don't want to give a compliment he didn't give me but it was something like, "Ah, I saw the last part of that, it was great." And then he walked by me and I was like, "Oh shit, Dave Chappelle." I'd paid to see Chappelle nine times. I saw him in the city all the time. It was just the first time here. It was like, "Dave Chappelle, this is Dan Soder," and then I proceeded to get drunk and he sat at the table. And John Mayer was there. It was very random. I was basically telling Chappelle how big of a fan I was and I got very drunk which I regret.

Author: Did you do anything stupid?

Dan: No. There was the coolest moment of my life though when Chappelle was sitting at the table. He had a cigarette as he always does and I asked him, I said, "Dave, I've always wanted to know," and this is true since I saw him for the first time when I was sixteen years old, I don't know if he smoked in that show, I think he started smoking later, but I said, "I've always wanted to know what kind of cigarettes you smoke." And he was like, "I smoke American Spirits." And I was like, "Oh, great." And he handed me one and I was like, "Oh, that's awesome, thanks." And I smoked at the time. I was like,

"Do you want to go outside and smoke?" And he was like, "We can smoke right here." And he smokes inside. There is no "go outside and smoke" for Dave Chappelle. So they get him a cup of water as an ashtray and then he lights his cigarette and I go, "You're Dave Chappelle, you can smoke in here, but I need this place for my rent." And he goes, "You can if Dave Chappelle lights your cigarette." And then he lit my cigarette and Estee gave me like a nod, "Yes, it's okay." And I took like maybe three pulls off it and I looked around and every waiter and the bartender, every waiter and waitress in that place, and the bartender, was just staring at me, like, "Are you fucking smoking in the Olive Tree?" I took maybe four drags and then I threw this cigarette out, because I didn't want to be disrespectful.

CHAPTER 120

John Cook reads an anonymous tip about Louis CK. He starts investigating. He starts writing a story. He discusses it with friends.

John: I had to kind of argue my way ... Not internally. Internally, everyone at *Gawker* was onboard, but just people I would talk to about this story, I had to sort of argue my way to seeing clear to do it, because there were a lot of people who were like, "Louis CK is on our side, why would you do this to one of ours?"

CHAPTER 119

Noam: Correlation is not causation. The trend was up all along and then the *Louie* show came along and we think that it had an impact as well. It clearly did have an impact but we can't be sure how much was the *Louie* show.

Author: No, sure. You can't get a number on that, but just, you're the owner of the club, I'm sure you have an instinct for how things are going.

Noam: We saw a lot of people coming in, a lot of people filming themselves doing the same opening that Louis did in his show. So we get the feeling that people are really into this show. And I think because Louis was so respected it was kind of a stamp of approval. Like, the greatest comic in the world had given his stamp of approval for this small club. So anybody who was into comedy … But this is how social media matters so much, because all the comedy aficionados from all over the world were really getting into comedy, like you. Like, you follow what's going on in the States now, right? That wasn't possible only a short while ago. You'd have no idea. So it just created this big audience, and not just out of the country but throughout the United States and everywhere. And YouTube, people were checking in on comedians and becoming fans of comedians and then they would google them and it would lead them to mentions of the Comedy Cellar, so it all was just, like, doubling up, you know, accelerating.

CHAPTER 118

Rick Crom: Everybody saw it. It suddenly became this internet sensation. And it got such great press, people like, "Oh my god, this is the most honest ten minutes in television." So I was sitting up here with my students and Louis walked in and he looked at me and said, "We made something good," or, "We did something good," I think that's what he said. I said, "Yeah, it's an amazing thing." And we started talking and one of my students who was drunk got up and tried to assault him or, you know, "I love you." Then we came over here and I said, "But I've got to tell you, I saw a couple of things in the gay press where the origin of the word 'faggot' is not what I said it was, but that's what I heard, it's a common story." And he looked at me and said, "That's fiction. The show is fiction. Don't worry about it." But I was worried. I thought, "Oh my god, they're going to get mad now."

CHAPTER 117

Before that, Louis uploads a scene from his new show onto YouTube,

Louis: Rick does it offend you when I say that word?

Rick: What word, "hello"?

Louis: No, "faggot."

Nick Di Paolo: Yeah, does it bother you when he says the word "faggot"?

Rick: No, it bothers me when you say it, because you mean it.

Louis: Yeah but really, as like, as a comedian and a gay guy, you're the only gay comic I know, do you think I shouldn't be using that word on stage?

Rick: I think you should use whatever words you want. When you use it on stage I can see it's funny and I don't care, but are you interested to know what it might mean to gay men?

Louis: Yeah, I am interested.

Rick: Well, the word "faggot" really means a bundle of sticks used for kindling in a fire. Now in the Middle Ages when they used to burn people they thought were witches, they used to burn homosexuals too. And they used to burn the witches at a stake but they thought the homosexuals were too low and disgusting to be given a stake to be burned on. So they used to just throw them in with the kindling with the other faggots. So that's how you get "flaming faggot."

Louis: So what you're saying is gay people are a good alternative fuel source.

Nick: That's how they get the term "diesel dyke."

Louis: I'm sorry, go ahead.

Rick: You might want to know that every gay man in America has probably had that word shouted at them when they're being beaten up, sometimes many times, sometimes by a lot of people all at once, so when you say it, it kind of brings that all back up. But you know, by all means use it, get your laughs, but now you know what it means.

CHAPTER 116

Author: I wondered how that came about? How he hired you for it? He seems to have hired lots of comedians from the Cellar for various things that he's done. Did he text you about it? Did he come and talk to you about it?

Rick: Well, here's what happened. The Comedy Cellar table back there had a certain vibe to it. So we would sit back there and the comedians, since I was the only openly gay guy they knew, they would ask me all sorts of questions about gay sex and stuff like that. I would tell them and when I would tell them they would squeal like little girls. Louis thought that was hilarious. So we'd do that.

Author: Who would ask you stuff?

Rick: Other comedians would ask things and bust your balls.

Author: Like Nick Di Paolo?

Rick: Nick Di Paolo. Just all the guys back then. And Jim Norton and all those guys. And then the story I told in the TV thing, the story about the jerk-off club, that's real. I told that story. It's a real place and they would ask me about it in terms of, "Well, what do you do?" And again I would very matter-of-factly tell them and I'm like, "You're the guys who keep bringing this up." It's like little kids, "I know this fire is hot but I want to touch it one more time." That and then the urban legend about the origin of the word "faggot" is something else that I'd said at the table. And that was just part of our conversation.

Author: Did Louis ask you about his use of the word "faggot" on the stage?

Rick: Yeah, but let me fill in one little gap with that history of the table back there. Louis is filming his first season, he's about eight episodes in. I happened to be here and hadn't been doing spots at the Cellar, but I'm hanging out. Louis sees me and he says, "Oh, hey. I want to ask you something." Okay. And he says, "You know those stories about the jerk-off club and the meaning of the word 'faggot', tell me those stories again." So I tell him the stories and he's asking me questions and he says, "I think I'm going to put those in the show. Do you want to play yourself?" I said, "Okay, sure." So he went away and a couple of days later I got a phone call, "Louis has written this scene. He wants to shoot it on Monday. Are you available?" "Yes, I'm available." So that scene, he took my stories and embellished them. The whole thing about the origin of the word, not the origin, but getting beat up and all that stuff. Now I never said any of that stuff. He made that up. Other people had said stuff. And he was going through a period at that time where he was getting flak for his "faggot" routine, for using the word, and he wanted to address that as part of the scene too. And I think he and I did have a talk about it. He did ask me, "Is it offensive?" I think he did. I think it was mostly like, "It depends on where it's coming from."

CHAPTER 115

Bonnie: I do remember once being at the Cellar table with the gang. I guess it was Bobby Kelly, Keith Robinson, Rich [her husband], Colin Quinn. I don't remember who was there. It was packed and they started making fun of me, which almost never happened. You know, that sort of bullying thing that they do.

Author: That sort of bullying thing.

Bonnie: It was relentless and I've been a part of it before but never quite getting this full tsunami of, you know, insults. And it was funny for a while.

Author: What was it about?

Bonnie: I don't remember. They just started making fun of me. I mean, it was like that was just standard practice. You just sort of found someone, someone who was weak, and this particular time it was me. And I was laughing at first. And then at some point it was like I just told myself, "Keep laughing," and then at one point Colin Quinn said, this is the only thing I really remember, Colin Quinn said, "The other night I bombed so hard I thought I was married to Rich Vos." And they were just unrelenting. I felt like, you know, you just have to sit there and get through it and hope it ends at some point, because I'm not easily offended, I don't have thin skin, but I remember being like, "Oh god, this is what it feels like when you're in it." It's just, you're fake laughing, "Oh very funny." The jokes start to get very like, "Alright, I get it, I bomb a lot."

Author: Is that something you're sensitive about? Like, bombing a lot?

Bonnie: Well this is the thing. When I got in the car to go home I was thinking, "Is that the thing that they think about me? Is that my character?" You learn a lot about yourself.

Author: So it hadn't occurred to you before?

Bonnie: I guess I didn't know that's what they ... I guess maybe I did. I do bomb.

Author: It's not something anybody's said to me about you, but basically, it's not something that had occurred to you before? But it got into your head?

Bonnie: I guess maybe I thought I'd been hiding that and now I was like, "They do know," because usually when I'm getting shit on, really they're just shitting on Rich through me. Like, "Why would you marry ..." Bad-taste-in-men kind of jokes. But this was really about me. And I swear, I think about that still every few days.

Author: Is that true? You really think about that?

Bonnie: I really do, because it's like one of those things. Like, that was my Vietnam. Like, I made it through. I'm tougher because of it. I'm a better person because of it.

Author: Did it particularly stick with you because ... I know you're fond of Colin, or I've heard you say on podcasts that you're very fond of Colin.

Bonnie: I love Colin, yeah. I love all those guys.

Author: Is that why it particularly stuck though? Because Colin's usually a really nice person, or he's often a very nice person when I see him. Is it because he decided to join in rather than it being like Sherrod or Jim Norton or someone like that?

Bonnie: No. I think … I don't … I think it's because it felt inclusive actually. You know, like, they didn't go soft on me at all. They weren't treating me with kid gloves in any way. They were just hammering on. And it was like, "I'm part of it. I'm in it."

CHAPTER 114

Andy de la Tour: You're actually told, you're under instruction, if you heckle you get thrown out, and it's quite aggressive that. Well, okay, but my experience of New York comedy by that time was that nobody heckles anyway. This is the most well-behaved audiences I've ever been to. That's one of the things people asked me when I came back, about it somehow being really, really difficult. The audiences were, I would say exclusively, every single space that I went to and the ones that I played were fantastically well behaved. Nobody heckled and shouted and stuff. Just nobody did that. You know, it was great. It's as it should be I suppose, but there was no sort of real danger. But I was also very … I'm remembering now. I was very disappointed by some of the stuff. That was a general observation about the stand-up in New York, but it's probably true of the stand-up in Britain, is that it's very mainstream, you know, it's become very, very mainstream. I mean, not overtly reactionary and racist, although some of it was and I was shocked by that. I think I mention that in the book.

Author: You do, and I wanted to ask you about that.

Andy: When I mention racist stereotypes, I was quite … As I'm talking now it's coming back to me. I was quite shocked about this whole thing about Mexicans and all that stuff. I thought, "Oh, here we go." We don't have "lazy Mexicans" in the UK. So this vein of humor seemed to be acceptable. I thought, "Oh, that's the situation is it now?" That the, as it were, so-called alternative scene has become the mainstream like it has in Britain of course years ago. So this stuff is now totally okay, to go on about this stuff and nobody would heckle? I was surprised. I mean, there was one particular comedian, I think he was the compere, who was coming out with this stuff, and I didn't heckle, but I tell you, I came bloody close to it. I came bloody close to it because I thought, "This is really out of order this stuff." Which is interesting because that touches into what you're talking about, what's allowable and what's not allowable. Well, one of the points I've made to people in the past, and I believe this, is that no-platforming comics to me is not acceptable, but if you don't like what they say, then heckle. Exercise your right to free speech to interrupt their right to free speech and see how they handle it.

Author: Well they get thrown out at the Comedy Cellar.

Andy: Well I think there's a really important distinction between that, because I think a comic should be allowed to say what he or she wants to say on stage. And that would include Bernard Manning. But their right to say that doesn't take away the right of an audience to respond to that if they don't like it. So to me, that's where I think free speech works. And in the stand-up comedy scene that's how it works. I don't think any comic should be banned. I don't think a comic should be blacklisted. I mean, for example, to go off the subject a bit, although it isn't really, the whole alternative comedy scene in the early Eighties arose out of a cultural reaction against the likes of Bernard Manning and co. That was a reaction against that kind of comedy. And the way you deal with that kind of comedy is you create your own. You create your own mores, you create your own comedy style, you create your own comedy in all the sense that means, but that's not calling for people to be banned or blacklisted because they're racist, you know. You answer it by dealing with it. You say, "This guy says this stuff, it isn't funny, but what we do is funny and we'll win the audience, and we'll win a bigger audience."

[After twenty-eight minutes]

Andy: Don't stand up in a public space and mouth off about something, it doesn't matter what your politics are, and then have a hissy fit if people answer back and say, "Well you're not supposed to do that, you're just supposed to pay and listen." You're up there showing off, you are, you're up there showing off, because you're up there telling the world, "This is what I think and this is worth listening to." So if somebody in the audience thinks, "This is actually not worth listening to, blah blah blah," then you have to deal with that. So if you're going to come out with material which you know is controversial, because most stand-up comedians, even if they're right-wing, are not complete idiots, if you're going to come up with stuff which you know is controversial, and somebody stands up and says something, then you have to have an answer to that. You have to deal with that. That's their right and so you have to deal with it. And if you're very good you deal with it and you come out on top because you have the microphone of course. So if people come out with some stuff and some person stands up and says, "You're a racist," then that person gets thrown out, it's completely out of order in my book, completely out of order.

CHAPTER 113

Greg Giraldo is dead.

Noam: He was one of the people my father really, really, really felt a strong closeness with.

Author: Why?

Noam: Because he was so smart and he also … They had some kind of connection. I remember, I have it somewhere, there was a big fight they had one time, where Giraldo was drunk, my father would have been drinking, they had a nasty fight and Giraldo said some stuff about Israel or something. I can't even remember, but then Giraldo wrote my father a two-page letter a few days later apologizing and expressing how much he loved my father and stuff like that, and my father was just so moved by that letter. He carried it around with him. He showed it to people who were close to him. It was very, very important to him. And sometimes a close bond is formed through arguments and bad things.

CHAPTER 112

Noam: I was going to run for Senate against Gillibrand in I guess 2010, and I had written to Pat Caddell about it, who was in the Jimmy Carter administration, and he's on TV a lot, and he asked me to ... He met with me and then he asked me to write something for him and I wrote him, like, where it's coming from, a summary of my positions and stuff. He was very impressed with it. He showed it to a lot of people. He showed it to Joe Trippe who was Howard Dean's campaign manager and I had some conversations with him. And then I had some conversations with Pat and I had a meeting with Dick Morris of all people, this is before Dick Morris was really untouchable, on the set of the *O'Reilly Factor*, but it never got off the ground because it was a little bit too late and raising the money was daunting.

CHAPTER 111

Noam emails the position summary to Pat,

My name is Noam Dworman and I want to be the next Senator from New York. The most important thing you need to know about me is that I'm not a politician, and that's exactly why I'm right for the job.

John Adams in his Thoughts on Government wrote that our legislature "should be in miniature an exact portrait of the people at large. It should think, feel, reason, and act like them." His point is so clearly correct, it would be hard to find anyone to dispute it. Nevertheless, we have suffered for years with an entrenched group of uninspired elitist politicians who clearly do not "think, feel and reason" like us. To be clear, this is a problem of both parties. We have for too long ignored Adams' advice, and we are suffering the consequences.

Let me tell you a little bit about myself. I'm a lifelong New Yorker with a very New York story. For twenty years I've been a small businessman running restaurants and nightclubs in Greenwich Village. I have an Ivy League law degree and I've served on my local community board. I'm a musician and a computer programmer. Between my wife and me, our family is a melting pot of Jewish, Puerto Rican, African American, and Indian. While the idea of me running for Senate may seem a bit crazy, I think there has never been a time when a citizen politician was more urgently needed. Our current leaders are out of ideas, and have failed us. It's time to consider other options.

Based on my experience, it is painfully obvious to me that we are moving in the wrong direction. Barack Obama has promised that he will "bring about the change that won't just win an election, but will transform America." He's not promising a "kinder, gentler" America, or a course correction, but a total transformation. Well I don't want to see America transformed.

I want to start by saying that I believe American ideas, American innovation, and American power have been the greatest forces for good in the history of the world. There is no person on earth who lives free, who does not in some way owe a debt of gratitude to the United States of America. In the twentieth century, in two world wars, and one cold war, it was America that stood between the world and tyranny. And now, in our war against terror, I believe historians will someday realize, we are doing so again. Virtually every major innovation, every great invention or industry of the last hundred years began in America. Like in the movie It's a Wonderful Life, *it's worth imagining what the world would be like if America had not existed. It's a frightening thought.*

America has transformed the world, yet now we are told that we are the ones that need to be transformed — as if we should repudiate and apologize for the last hundred years of American history. I believe this is a terrible mistake. We have our problems, as every generation has had its unique problems, but the answer has always been the same. Yes, it is essential to make sure that our financial markets are better regulated. But even more urgently, we need to unleash the creative and innovative forces of the American people. We must set government on a fiscally responsible path and move aggressively to remove the barriers that are preventing us from achieving the greatness that used to come to us so easily.

It's fashionable in certain circles to believe that our best days are behind us. New York construction workers built the Empire State Building in just one year and forty-five days using 1920s technology, during a recession. Yet today, almost ten years later there is still a hole at Ground Zero.

In a different time our leaders would have rebuilt the towers and added a few extra stories as a message to our enemies: we will not be defeated. Today, we accept paralysis as a fact of life. We have to ask ourselves: are we ready to accept that America can no longer build Empire State Buildings? Are we ready to accept that we can no longer land men on the moon? Have we psychologically accepted that we are a nation in decline? For if we have, it will certainly become a self-fulfilling prophecy.

I don't think Americans are ready to accept our decline. We need to turn things around, and we need to start by cleaning house. We hire our legislators for a term, and at the end of that term we are almost universally dissatisfied with their results. Then rather than hold them accountable, we routinely re-elect them for another term. This brings to mind the classic definition of mental illness: doing the same thing over and over and expecting a different result. We are not going to get a different result unless we do things differently.

Many may call me too inexperienced for the job of Senator. On the contrary, it is our current crop of legislators who lack the necessary experience to do their jobs well. Most of our legislators are either lawyers or career politicians — a scant few have ever held a real job let alone had to meet a payroll. I believe that the people who make the laws should have had experience living and working under them. We have a ruling class in our country that give the illusion of experience and competence, but actually have neither. A ruling class that claims to be fighting unemployment while they wage war on the only people who can actually create a job — employers.

Small businesses are the biggest employers in America. You want a small business owner to hire more people? Easy. Let him keep his money and use it to grow his business. Business owners are after all dreamers. They had an idea, and they've taken an enormous risk to see it come true. They view their businesses as an extension of themselves, and are always

190

looking to improve them. Every extra dollar that they don't pay in taxes is a dollar that they can use to hire a new worker, give raises, increase hours, start renovations, and use to expand their business. But what do our experienced legislators do? They tax business to the bone, add on fees, fines, surcharges and penalties, while at the same time saddling them with the bureaucratic burdens of collecting child support, withholding taxes, garnishing wages, and now administering the health insurance of all its employees. The ease with which the government saddles business owners with an ever-growing list of responsibilities and costs is stupefying, until you realize that the people making these laws have never run a business themselves. They don't know what they are doing. They are the ones without experience.

Senators with the proper life experiences are essential to good government. George McGovern after retiring from the Senate went into the inn business. His experience caused him to rethink the laws he had supported. "If I were back in the US Senate or in the White House," he wrote, "I would ask a lot of questions before I voted for any more burdens on the thousands of struggling businesses across the nation." And let's remember that the burdens on business he dealt with in his day were minuscule compared to the ones that Washington is now planning.

It is not reasonable to fight unemployment by fighting employers. Let's remember — despite what they take credit for, no president has ever created a job.

If the current healthcare bill is not drastically altered, it threatens to be the final knife in the back of small businesses. Businesses with more than fifty employees will now be required to provide health insurance to its employees, or pay a $2,000 fine per employee. And, if you have two businesses with let's say twenty-six employees each, the government will consider it as one business (never mind that each business has its own rent and expenses, or that they may not both be profitable). So if *you employ fifty-one people, you can either pay $102,000 in fines, or pay who knows how much for healthcare. $102,000 is enough money to put many small businesses out of business. This is the greatest tax on small business ever conceived. Yet the government claims it cares about unemployment. As I've said, our leaders, having never run anything but a campaign, have no experience; they don't know what they're doing. It's time to elect someone who does.*

Leaving aside the burden on small business, they have made a drastic mistake in the healthcare bill. How can Congress arrogantly pass a three-thousand-page bill that they haven't even read, revamping one-sixth of our GDP, and really expect it to be anything but a disaster? Any business owner knows how difficult it is to accomplish even small things well. Only the inexperienced think they can wish something and make it so. Anybody who thinks that the cost of this plan will not be at least two or three times the current projections is living in a dream world.

And amazingly, the plan offers absolutely no mechanisms to stem the growth of healthcare costs. The problem with health insurance costs is contained in the very nature of insurance: once you pay the upfront pre-mium, your incentive is to get as much in return as possible. You don't care what the medical treatment is costing, and have absolutely no reason to watch what you spend — so of course prices soar. We need a system which uses competition to drive medical costs down. Consumers must have an incentive to compare prices. Supercomputers have gone from hundreds of thousands of dollars, to less than one hundred. GPS satellites can guide your car from outer space for $50. The American free enterprise system has produced miracle after miracle, why wouldn't it have the same effect on healthcare? It seems our leaders have lost faith in competition.

Consider that the cost of Lasik eye surgery has dropped from tens of thou-sands of dollars to hundreds of dollars. Why? Because it is not usually covered by insurance, so people shop for the best price. Competition will work, but it will take experimentation, and the flexibility to allow states to try various ideas until a superior system can emerge. In my view a little trial and error is required — nobody is smart enough to figure it all out at once. In the meantime, the healthcare bill needs to be severely scaled back or repealed. To start, in addition to competition across state lines, tort reform, and other ideas that can help control costs, I would propose a means-tested national catastrophic healthcare plan. Nobody should lose everything they have because they get sick.

We need safety nets we can afford, and those who can afford it may not really need a safety net. I agree that the wealthy can afford to pay higher taxes. I don't object to millionaires paying a higher amount into social security. No matter how you explain it, Warren Buffet should not be paying a lower tax rate than his secretary. This must be addressed. But a family earning $200,000 in New York is not Warren Buffet. And if that family owns a business, every additional dollar we tax is one less dollar available to hire an additional worker.

We have to understand that no matter how much revenue the government has, it will never be enough. I believe this is a fundamental principle. Expenditures will always rise to meet any level of revenue. And once they are instituted, every expenditure becomes essential, and can't be cut in leaner times. Floridians pay something like half the taxes that New Yorkers do, yet they receive equivalent government services — they find a way to make do with less.

We must reject ever-increasing taxation as a solution. In my view, it is morally wrong to expect anybody to pay more than half his income to the government. People should not have to spend most of their time working for the state. And in New York, between state, local, federal, fees, sales taxes, many New Yorkers are paying upwards of sixty-five per cent of their income to the government. Yet it's still not enough. We need to keep taxes at a reasonable rate and cut government to live within its means.

President Obama had promised to end earmarks, yet the stimulus bill contained nine thousand of them. While it's true that the sum total of these earmarks will not significantly affect our deficits, any hard-earned dollar that is taken from us and then put to a corrupt use is an outrage. Who could not be angered to know that their tax dollars went to study swine manure management or tattoo removal for gang members? We work extremely hard to earn this money; our government should not be so comfortable squandering it.

In foreign affairs I support the president in his desire to have good relations with all foreign governments. Our president is a gifted man, and a wonderful ambassador to the world. Nevertheless I think we need to remember who are our friends, and who are our enemies. Let's not forget who was crying when the towers came down, and who was cheering. 9/11, which was the defining moment of the twenty-first century, occurred only a year after Israel had accepted the Clinton plan for peace in the Middle East. It was the Palestinians who rejected it without so much as a counter proposal, and then initiated a bloody intifada. And as far as I know, they haven't changed their minds or expressed regret at their decision. Yet lately we have come perilously close to blaming the Israelis for our problems in the Middle East. But how long should we expect Israel to tie up its flexibility, its freedom to act the way every other nation on earth can, in servitude of a lie — the lie that they have a partner for a two-state solution peace? It is a lie, and we should say so. I have spent my entire life socializing, playing music and working with Arabic people, and I have an admiration and love for them. Yet I think it's clear that the Palestinians are not rejecting peace because Israel has plans to build some apartments in a Jewish neighborhood in Jerusalem.

In the Middle East, we may be living in 1939 all over again. Iran has made its intentions every bit as clear as Mein Kampf, *yet we seem to be drifting towards acceptance of an Iranian nuclear bomb. We can't let this happen.*

The belief that we could change Iran by talking to them more nicely was dangerously naive. We and our allies need to be prepared to impose tough sanctions against the Iranians, with or without the UN — and we must not appear to take the military option off the table. We need to set out what the consequences will be if Iran continues its policies, and those consequences need to be severe. We may not have any perfect options in Iran, however we should not forget that even imperfect measures can slow Iran's nuclear progress. Iran is a politically unstable regime, and time may present us with future opportunities that are currently unforeseeable.

And we need to get off foreign oil — and fast. As George Will has pointed out, China begins construction on a new nuclear plant every three months, while we have not built a new one in thirty years. I'm all for exploring and supporting other forms of alternative energy, but how about utilizing the one that is proven and available? The combination of nuclear produced energy and electric cars can revolutionize our environment and our foreign problems. The President seems fond of European ideas; eighty per cent of France's electricity is produced through nuclear power. If we are not aggressively pursuing nuclear power, we are not truly serious about energy policy.

CHAPTER 110

Author: The place had developed this reputation for being where the comedians wanted to hang around. There was a table for them and it was a good atmosphere, then you kind of took it over. Did you worry about keeping that atmosphere? Did you worry about what kind of relationship you would have with the comics?

Noam: I did worry about it. I worried about not wanting to appear this young kid who inherits a club and then tries to say, "Okay, I'm the new …" To step into my father's shoes and expect them to … I was always worried about that.

CHAPTER 109

Noam: I always knew that he was leaving half to me and half to Ava. And he was concerned about there being ... Two people running a business together is a common way to cause a lot of disagreement between two people. So he was concerned about it becoming an issue in my relationship with Ava, because we have a very good relationship. So he would try to give us advice about that. But he didn't encourage me to take more interest in the Comedy Cellar. I think he figured that I had the Cafe Wha and I had that other stuff, and that Ava would basically run the Olive Tree and the Comedy Cellar day to day, and that's how it would be.

Author: Okay. So after he had died, did Ava run the Comedy Cellar?

Noam: She did, but Ava has no interest really in show business and so ...

Author: She was a teacher?

Noam: No that was a different wife of his. I'm sorry to confuse you. No, her name was Carol. Ava he got with later, when I was already in law school.

Author: What did she do?

Noam: She used to work as a bartender and then as a manager of the

Olive Tree, and she's an artist.

Author: Did your wife work as a bartender?

Noam: Yes, my wife worked as a waitress around seventeen years ago.

Author: Like father like son.

Noam: Like father like son, right.

Author: So Ava wasn't interested in the Comedy Cellar really, so who was running it?

Noam: She was running it. She was interested in it, she just didn't get any joy out of the fact it was a comedy club, you know, and she was doing most of her work during the day, and Estee was taking care of most of the booking and stuff like that at night, and that's the way we went on for a few years.

Author: And what kind of form did your resistance take? You just didn't hang around there? Did you find the comedians difficult?

Noam: No, I didn't have any bad feelings about it. It kind of went back to what I had said to you before. I didn't see the Comedy Cellar as a vehicle for me to … It was a fully cooked idea. It was successful. It was nothing that needed any improvement. And the real talent was the comedians. So, you know, it was hard to get all excited about getting involved in it.

Author: So why did you start getting involved it? Was there a trigger?

Noam: Yeah, the main trigger was that Ava was getting totally burnt out, and she's a very fine artist, and she was not able to find the time to paint or draw anything for years. So I told her that I would take it over.

CHAPTER 108

Author: But at some point you were passed at the Cellar, do you know when?

Joe DeRosa: Yeah, that was about seven days in 2007. It was so brief I don't even remember. Honestly I don't even remember. I was passed there … The first time I auditioned I didn't pass.

Author: Was that with Estee?

Joe: Yeah, yeah. It was always her as long as I can remember. First time I went up where I didn't pass. The second time was years later. It's funny too, when you don't pass … Just to get the audition means you have to be recommended by a regular there, and somebody that she likes quite a bit, enough to call in that favor. And it also means that you know people think you're ready to jump into the quote big room unquote, and you know, so you go in and everybody's like cheering you on. And then you bomb and then nobody talks to you. I just remember leaving that place like I had the fucking plague that night. It's like, yeah, where did all the love go everybody?

Author: So that was the first time you auditioned. That was in 2007?

Joe: I honestly can't remember. It was probably, oh god, I don't know, it was probably four years after I was in New York something like that. Four or five years. The funny thing is I got the audition because somebody fell out one night and they were in a jam, and they said, "Put Joe on, he's funny." And I went on and I did really well that night. That was a late night spot. It was like 1am. And I did well. And the staff, everybody was like, "Man, you should be working here." And then when I went up in front of Estee I just choked. I bombed.

Author: And who was it who recommended you, was it Robert Kelly?

Joe: No, Lynne Koplitz recommended me the first time. Bobby recommended me the second time.

Author: And do you know when was the second time?

Joe: That was … that was a couple of years after that first thing, because you've got to kind of let the smell dissipate after you stink the place up.

Author: When you said there was a lot of love the first time you auditioned but then it didn't go well, do you remember walking up to the table to sit back down? Or did you just leave straight away? Did anyone say anything?

Joe: No. Lynne said something to me when I was done, but I could tell it was like, she knew I bombed. I knew I bombed. It was just like, "Good job." She was being nice. She was being sweet and supportive, but we both knew I ate my fucking ass. And that was that. I remember leaving. Just kind of leaving. There were no two ways about it. I didn't do what I needed to do.

Author: Then a couple of years later Robert Kelly recommended you to Estee again and you auditioned and it went well?

Joe: In a rare stroke of genius I chose to open with the same joke I had opened with two years earlier, just to shoot myself in the foot I guess. So that almost cost me the second audition.

Author: Did Estee say something about that?

Joe: Yeah, yeah, she almost … She was just about to walk out and Bobby was like, "No, no, no, just watch him, just watch him." So she did and I did okay and she passed me. And, you know, from there on out it's the story that a lot of people have. I worked there for a little while, doing late night spots, a couple of weeks or whatever. And then you just suddenly … You don't get spots. And I guess it just wasn't in my … I mean, for me it was a thing … I saw … I won't name names but I saw people that worked there that were really, really affected by that, and really got into this headspace of like, "Well, why am I not getting booked right now?" And, "Oh, I'm back in." It was almost like a barometer for how they felt about their career or something.

Author: Yeah, it does seem that way.

Joe: And I kind of saw that and, you know, whatever it was about that, I just didn't like … I just didn't want to feel that way. And look, that could have just been a … That could have just been an excuse for me to not have to go back ever again, because I still found the place terribly intimidating, and it still made me nervous, and you know … It just … I just never fully felt comfortable there. So whether or not that was the best thing for me to do, I don't know, but I just decided …

Author: You seem to have done alright.

Joe: Well, I just basically decided I don't want to feel that way. I don't want a club to get in my head that way. So they seemed to have stopped using me and slowly I stopped calling in avails. And that was that. But who knows, they might never have wanted to use me again anyway. So I have no idea.

CHAPTER 107

Author: I don't know if you remember this, but there was a meeting between the comedians and the club owners.

Noam: Yeah, I remember. At the Friars Club.

Author: Yes, and so some of the comedians told me that at one point you said ... You were talking about the risk that the Comedy Cellar takes, that of course you make money, but you always take a lot of the risk. For example, if the club's closed for the weekend due to bad weather you said you'd be missing out on ... And nobody remembers what the amount was but they were all like, "What? You make that?" They were shocked that you made that much money in a weekend. Does that ring a bell at all?

Noam: No, but it sounds like me, because, first of all, these guys are unbelievable. It is simple arithmetic. Any of the Jewish comedians could have told you exactly what I was making on a weekend, because you know how many seats there are, you know how much the cover charge is, and you know how much a drink is, so on the back of a matchbook anybody, anybody, a high school kid, a grammar school kid, could come up with a pretty good estimation of what the club takes in. What they don't have any idea of is the expenses. What's the rent? What's the electricity? What's the insurance? What's the payroll? What's the mortgage? I mean, that they have no idea about, but the fact that whatever the number was that ... The Comedy

Cellar had a $10 cover charge at the time, times a hundred seats, let's say times three shows on a Friday and four shows on a Saturday, I think that's what it was, plus maybe $20 a person in drinks. Add it up. That's what we were taking in.

Author: I think someone said $30k or something like that?

Noam: In a weekend? Between Friday and Saturday night? No, I think it would be a little less than that. I think it would have been more like $25,000 between the two nights in 2004. But that's gross and that includes sales tax by the way. It's a meaningless number. I do remember other things about the meeting that I pointed out to them, that I thought that their whole calculation was … I don't remember what word I used, but I'm trying to put a word on it now for what my intention was. That it was naive, in the sense that Gotham has three-hundred-and-fifty seats or something. We have a hundred seats. We're using six or seven comics a night. Other places are using two or three comics a night. So the overall … They were comparing spot pay rather than comparing the overall budget for comedy. And then, even further, the overall budget for comedy as a percentage of the gross of that particular room. Almost like comparing a guy who pays $2,000 rent to a guy who pays $20,000 dollars rent without talking about the fact that yeah, but his place is twice as big, his location is better, whatever. So we were not only paying the most for a spot but we were by far using the most comedians. And I think I remember saying at the meeting, "Look, would you prefer I use fewer comedians?" And everyone was like, "No, no, no." They didn't want that. So we felt that even at lower pay we were way superior to the other clubs because we were paying much more in absolute dollars and we had many fewer seats. You follow me, right? So this was my recollection, and I think when I said all that, these are smart guys, the comedians, I think most of them said, "Oh yeah, he has a point, we still want more money."

CHAPTER 106

Before that, Russ Meneve emails hundreds of New York comedians,

Fellow comedians, I am sending you this letter to give you the opportunity to address the weekend spot pay in New York City. Every comedian reachable will receive this letter as you have; based on the responses a meeting will be scheduled. If there is little response to this, then it will certainly stop here. However, if you share our concerns, Ted Alexandro and myself are ready and willing to organize the effort. Unfortunately, it is a necessary burden in business to negotiate prices, salary, etc. A burden we simply do not address as a group which has resulted in the very low pay we are getting. I want to say categorically, the club owners are not to blame. History has shown that in every situation similar to this the owners will try to raise profits to the disadvantage of the service-providing group, until the group demands a change. It is inherent in the situation. With laborers mainly, in addition to every sport where the money is mathematically undeniably there, management tries to pay as little as possible to the worker or athlete until demands are made. I'll never forget what a New York club owner said to me when he was talking about the comedy business — one point he made was, "You can't let the people in without a cover charge or a charge that is too low, or they will not respect the show." In essence, it is the reason we are treated the way we are. There is little respect for us and our challenges because we give our product away for so little. We don't even make a real demand for a more than fair pay raise in the course of twenty years. Think of how many years it took each of us to get to the skill level required at this point. Do you not respect this, what you've done? Can you evoke the difficulty in doing so, let alone the pain endured? Really think about the hardship you went through, and respect it because it is something special. I am certainly not asking for anything unfair, the cost of living has substantially increased in twenty years, which goes without saying. The cover charges and drinks have increased substantially, and the people are certainly turning out to the shows. But I think the lack of consideration for us, particularly in the wake of a recent twenty-five per cent cab fare increase, needs to be addressed. The club owners are very aware of how little we're making, certainly they are aware of the very large cab increase (a very high cost we must absorb on a weekend running to spots). I just wonder what the thought process was when they learned of this? Does it baffle you that they could not come to our aid in the least, since they are paying us so little already? One point that was made to me many years ago by a club owner was, "Well, when you make it big are you going to give me any of your money?" May I simply address this point by stating the unfortunate odds of this business, perhaps less than one per cent of us will make it to the kind of level they are implying. However, all of us can make reasonable livings as comedians since there is an obvious market for it. Making a living is a business; we must negotiate our product fairly. I wondered and laughed if this attempt I'm making to better the situation fails because of a lack of solidarity amongst the comics. Will it be the year 2050 and comics will be saying, "Hey, can you believe we're getting the same pay they did in '85? Sixty-five years man, this is wrong! Well, I gotta go, I have a spot." Again, I am not blaming the club owners. It is a natural progression from their side, which should lead to one on ours. It is simply business, and negotiation is a critical part of it as in all businesses. The fact that we have not seriously done it is our own fault and the reason we are in this position. Please let me know your thoughts, I truly believe this can be worked out with the best feelings on both ends as a result.

CHAPTER 105

Months earlier, Noam types what he'll say,

Good afternoon. First on behalf of Ava and myself let me thank you all not only for coming today, but for the utter devotion so many of you showed to my father during the months of his illness. You truly were a comfort. We are all very sad today. My father, through the brute force of his talent, intellect and personality altered the course of so many people's lives. He was many things, a gifted musician, a unique entertainer, a brilliant thinker capable of penetrating original insights. He was also extremely critical in judgments, but when he admired people, he went all out to tell them of it. And because there was no deception in him, his praise meant more than anyone else's. How many of us would be the same today, in careers, in our families, in our knowledge, in our outlooks and beliefs if we had not encountered his life, and his creations. I, of course, can't even imagine how I would be. I learned almost everything I know from my father. I had guitar teachers, but I learned to be a musician in our living room. I went to law school, but I had already been taught logical thinking at our dinner table. I've read countless books on business, but none of them has imparted anything more than my father's constant adage, you give good, you get good. As my father liked to say, all the rest is commentary. My father also taught me to value my own happiness in life. He pressured me heavily to go to law school, but when it turned out that I didn't enjoy the practice, he embraced my decision to give it up. He was flexible enough to recognize that my happiness should always come first. There were other lessons. A funeral is no time to avoid the truth, and as many of you know, my father never held his tongue, especially at funerals. So let me tell you that my father was fond of bragging that he had taught me by example to stay away from marijuana and having too many girlfriends. In fact, I think he tried to teach us all that. My father definitely did not believe in life after death or karma. He would dismiss those notions as flaky, or supernatural. But as I said, he did believe that if you give good, you get good, which, I think, is really as succinct a definition of karma as anyone has ever offered. Still, for many of you who might believe that a man's fortune in life is impacted by his goodness, it should be very easy to deduce that my father was a very good man. He had success and happiness in everything he endeavored. He loved his life, and never more than in his final years, enjoying the enormous success of the Comedy Cellar, and sitting at the table with his adopted second family, his beloved comedians. Even in the nature of his death he was fortunate. He had almost no suffering. And, although cancer ravaged his body, it left his mind and amazingly his remarkable sense of humor intact. He was fortunate in that he did not die suddenly. He had time to have his final words with all his old friends and associates. He had the opportunity to fully express his feelings to his wife, Ava, and, most importantly for me, he and I had the time to settle our differences, which were minor, and affirm our love for each other which endures. He was able to die with a peaceful mind, and I am able to live with one. He thus left me with a precious gift which not every son receives. I think one can see the goodness and gain insight into my father's character by hearing the things he worried about in his final months. Even when things like money could no longer make a difference to him, he worried about the health and vibrancy of his businesses. From his hospital bed, he worried about the hummus in his last week with the same intensity that he would have twenty years ago. Some of you may have never fully understood this about him, but making money was never important to my father. Never. It was his artistic creations, his businesses, that he worried about. Their health was an end in itself. Money, my father used to say, was a fortunate by-product, not a motiva-

tion. He worried about his dog Belle, and whether she had her step pillow that she needed to get on and off the couch without help. He worried about Israel and the future of the Jewish people. A recent conversation on the subject moved him to tears. Still, at the same time he took enormous pride in the devotion he was shown by so many of the Arabic people with whom he had worked. He loved them. They knew very well how my father felt about the most important issues in their lives, yet they adored him in return. This was also one of my father's remarkable gifts. He worried about his integrity, about having done the right thing, this was very important to him. He worried about me and Ava, intensely. He made us take an oath that we would always stay together and care for each other. He spent almost no time worrying about himself. He was remarkably brave. They say there are supposed to be five stages to death, denial, anger, and so on. Not so. With my father there was only one, acceptance, and he reached it on day one. With him, human psychology was no match for the logic of the situation. Finally, if any more indication was needed of my father's goodness, how else can one explain that he was able to earn the boundless love of someone as good as Ava? My father would never forgive me if anyone were to leave here today without knowing that Ava did not leave his side once, not once, not even for a short time during the last three months of his life. She took care of his most intimate needs, and, as he put it to me, did things which no one should have to do, and she did them happily, and she did them with love. I've tried to come up with the proper words to describe her devotion, but I really can't. No one can. We tend to use the word love trivially and casually in even the most minor relationships. But there is simply no word in the English language to describe the self-sacrifice she has shown him. I had a thought, that just as the Eskimo language has ten words to describe the various types of snow, English needs a word reserved simply for this most unusual and selfless type of love, a love which is seen only rarely, like great genius is seen only rarely, a love in a sense defiant of nature, in that it develops not between a parent and child, not based on blood or biology, but between strangers, a man and a woman who meet by chance. When it comes to Ava, I think the English language falls short. The love between a parent and child is easier to understand. Still, no son could be more sure of a father's love than I. Even as a small child I knew it was special. Many fathers with much more free time and much less responsibility routinely leave their children. My father swore never to leave me. While my father was sick, I was reminded bittersweetly of so many memories. When I felt his head for a fever, I remembered how he would check my head for a fever, and how his hand felt. When he was undergoing a painful procedure, I remembered how, when I was young, he had once intervened to prevent a doctor from hurting me, and to let me catch my breath, but this time I couldn't protect him as he had protected me. And as New Year's Eve approached I remembered how every year at midnight he would come over to the Wha to hug me and kiss me, and how during years we were fighting, I dreaded the arrival of midnight, because I knew he wouldn't be coming. And I knew he must have been suffering as well. All those things are behind me now, and all of us. I mentioned, my father always claimed that he did not believe in life after death, but of course even he didn't know for sure. Still, today, after the burial, many of us will come back to the Olive Tree to sit together and reminisce. We'll sit in that beautiful room which he built, with its beautiful colors, the stained glass ouds and star of David, Ava's wonderful drawings, Charlie Chaplin on the screen, and in the background we'll hear the laughter of the comedians and his music playing, in essence an enduring mosaic of my father's life and his interests, and we can take comfort that in this world, the existence of which we can all be sure of, he has in essence achieved his immortality. Thank you all for coming.

CHAPTER 104

Mohamed El-Taweel: He's in the bed, I swear to god, he told me, "Take care of the chicken." Do you believe it? He said to take care of the chicken. The man's finished. Tomorrow he dies and he still worry about the chicken.

CHAPTER 103

Noam: It had actually metastasized to his brain.

CHAPTER 102

Noam: But it started with lung cancer.

CHAPTER 101

Noam: He had been a heavy cigarette smoker until I guess he was fifty, around fifty, so the doctors seemed to think that probably had the biggest impact.

CHAPTER 100

Noam: I remember saying to him that I thought the Comedy Cellar was going to go downhill. I said, "Well, *Tough Crowd* will eventually get canceled."

Author: How did you know it was going to get canceled?

Noam: Everything eventually gets canceled. And Seinfeld's documentary was over and I just felt we'd had a lot of lucky breaks all in a row, and our luck was going to run out, and then the Comedy Cellar would dissipate.

CHAPTER 99

Author: You said there was a period when you'd fallen out with your dad, and at New Year's Eve you hated it because you knew he wasn't going to come over and say Happy New Year like you used to, but then you made up with him before he died. But I just wondered what it was that you fell out about?

Noam: Oh it was over some business stuff. Stupid stuff.

Author: Was he disagreeing with what you were doing at the Cafe Wha or was it to do with money?

Noam: It wasn't to do with money. He was worried. He didn't like for whatever reason that I was expanding at the Village Underground and Fat Black Pussycat. And to this day I don't know why he took it to the extreme that he did. I don't know, but it became very ugly between us. And looking back on it, it's so stupid. It's not like anybody ever did anything to anybody. There was never one of these stories of betrayal from one party to another. There was nothing like that. It was really just … I don't know. It was just a small thing which got blown out of proportion. I don't know why.

Author: Things like that happen in families don't they. Did you literally not speak to him for a long time?

Noam: We were never not talking, but it became very, you know, very short, tense conversations.

Author: And in the end it seems to me you demonstrated that the Village Underground could succeed as a music club and Fat Black Pussycat could succeed as a bar, but was that before he died or did you never get to demonstrate to him that they were viable businesses?

Noam: Yeah, they were both viable before he died, especially the Fat Black Pussycat. Yeah, I don't know. Ava could probably tell you better. I don't know if she wants to talk about that. She had his ear at the time in a way that I didn't and, you know, I don't really go into it with her, so I don't know.

Author: Before he died did he ever actually say, "Noam, you did well"? Was there any kind of making amends like that?

Noam: Just to be clear, I don't think it's because he didn't think I could run the businesses. That's what's weird about it. He just didn't like the idea that I had these businesses. He didn't expect me to fail I don't think. That wouldn't have made him angry. So, no. When he was sick at the end he made remarks like, you know, it was clear that this didn't matter at that point.

CHAPTER 98

Ava: He bought every newspaper because he liked to know all the different …

Noam: The *Times*, the *Post*, whatever news magazines.

Ava: And when he used to speak with the comedians when they talked about politics and stuff, he'd give them things to read.

Noam: Sometimes he'd buy them all a copy of the same book and tell them, "I want you to read this and then we'll talk about it. You're not ready to talk about this. You don't know what you're talking about."

Ava: But he would talk about both sides of it, the Left and the Right side, so he wanted to see the whole picture.

Author: Can you think of a book he did that with?

Noam: Yeah, *The Case for Israel* by Alan Dershowitz. He must have bought fifty copies of that book.

Ava: And then on the other hand when a book came out … I don't know if you remember, Benny something or other.

Noam: Benny Morris, *Righteous Victims*.

Ava: Which questioned the history of Israel, he was the first one to say it, and it upset Estee and a lot of people, because he was giving the other point of view.

CHAPTER 97

Colin: He'd be like, "Let me ask you something, why do you believe Palestine? Okay, now let me ask you this. What are you basing that on?" So he'd be very logical. He'd be, like, "Well are you talking about …" And you'd be like, "Oh, I don't know." And he'd go, "So if you don't know then why would you come to that conclusion?"

CHAPTER 96

Colin: You'd come in and he'd be like, "Listen, I want you to read this." Noam does too with these young guys. "I want you to read this," it was before email really, "And I'm going to come back and I'm interested to see what you think of this, because I'll tell you what I think when you read it." And then you read it and you sit around and have these, like, Socratic ... He loved ideas.

Author: You said when you first came to the Cellar it was an amazing place. You loved it straight away and then it started to be like the Left Bank in Paris, these chain-smoking Israelis talking about deep stuff.

Colin: Right, it's always what I envisaged the Village would be, you know.

Author: Did you read the stuff that he asked you to read?

Colin: Of course. We were very close. He liked to talk. He liked to make you talk. He was like that. That's why I say, like, Socratic ... He's like, "What do you think about that?" And that's how Noam is too. "Okay, I understand that, what is the answer?" And he's just like his father in that way, he wants to probe, but he's not trying to catch you. He's not trying to win. He's trying to find that essential truth to things, and if you have it then he's more than happy to hear it.

CHAPTER 95

Author: What did Manny say?

Louis CK: He said, "You're an idiot." I said, "Why do you just say I'm an idiot?" And he said, "Did you hear Bush say that we're doing it for oil? Did he say that?" I said, "No, of course he didn't." He said, "Then you're just a fucking idiot because can you read inside of a person's mind? Is this something that you know about him?" "No, but look, he has an oil company and he invaded an oil country." He's like, "Do you hear what an asshole and an idiot you sound like? You don't know these things." He said, "Limit yourself to the things that you know about this person and things that he has represented. You don't think you can argue there? You don't think that you have enough?" So I refocused my argument and I remembered that Bush had said that he was doing this war to promote democracy and the thing was that they weren't letting any parties run in the elections really that they didn't like, so I said, "I think it's bullshit that it's for democracy." And he said, "There you have an argument."

Author: Right. So this was probably 2003?

Louis: So I think it was Bush, the second Bush perpetrating the war after 9/11, I think that's what it was. But it informed my thinking because you can just drink a beer and talk shit, but if you really want to get to the bottom of something you engage with what people are actually saying, and it's usually enough. And I wish people thought like that more. People create a fake person out of somebody like a politician, they create their own image, and then they argue with that, and it gets you nowhere. So anyway. And you could extrapolate that to a lot of things, not just politics. Having a little more civility to your thinking by dealing with reality.

CHAPTER 94

Jim Norton: Manny is the only non-comedian, he literally could have a table of comedians shut the fuck up and listen to him. It's amazing. Everyone respected him, not because he was the owner, but because he was really funny and really smart, and he was very considerate in his arguments, and very, very ferocious, and he would yell. I saw him, one time I was at the table and Manny and somebody were talking about the Middle East. And Manny, he loved to argue about the Middle East. And good luck debating that with him. And somebody listening at the bar overheard. It might have even been me and Manny debating something, but not even that passionately because I knew Manny knew way more than I did about that shit. I only played devil's advocate. And the guy at the bar goes, "I don't agree with that." And Manny goes, "What do you mean you don't agree with it?" You know, Manny was drinking, and the guy goes, "I just don't." And Manny's like, "Well, come over, defend yourself." And the guy's like, "Nah, I don't want to get involved." And Manny goes, "You're a coward." And he starts screaming at this customer, it's his fucking customer, this maniac is yelling, and then Manny goes, "Oh, I'll buy you a drink. I own this place." And the guy goes, "Who the hell are you?" "I own this place." So he gets the guy to come over and sit down and have a drink and in ten minutes they're friends.

CHAPTER 93

Greg Giraldo types a letter,

My dearest Manny,

I don't quite know where to begin. You should know that as I write this I am sick to my stomach with shame.

Before I even begin to address the situation as Colin described it to me, I want to say some things that may be easier to express in writing and that hopefully will make clear that there was nothing underlying my moronic antics other than blind drunkenness.

First of all, Manny, you should know how incredibly highly I think of you. Our relationship has become, quite honestly, one of the most important in my life. You are one of the most interesting, intelligent and funny guys I've ever known. The friendship, support, inspiration and generosity you've shown me has affected me more deeply than you might even imagine.

Obviously, you know how much I like, admire and respect you. But perhaps you don't know how deeply my feelings run. Hearing that I may have done or said anything that caused you any serious displeasure or that made you question my feelings toward you in any way has quite literally made me sick. I know we'll be talking about this in person and I hope to be able to set things as straight as possible then, but I do want to talk about the general situation a little. Knowing you, I assume that you lend little credence to the notion that a drunk fool could spew completely meaningless bullshit. Colin and I discussed the fact that you are likely to think that what I said and did must have come from some real place, that I must have feelings beneath the surface that came to light in my drunkenness. Again, after talking to Colin, I only vaguely remember the specific things I said. But I hope you'll believe me when I say from the bottom of my heart that I have absolutely no unresolved issues with you. I have nothing but positive and warm feelings for you. I love the discussions that we have. I was so happy with this whole book thing that I was going to suggest we all make it a habit to read the same things at the same time, etc. I think you're always willing to listen to all perspectives and in fact are only too often frustrated that no one is able to provide a sufficiently challenging argument for you. Colin told me that the word "Nazi" came up. The fucking stupidity of that is so obvious that I almost can't think of what to say about it.

Colin also said that you felt betrayed, that there was something in my tone and demeanor which implied that I had anger toward you for some reason, or that I was trying to embarrass you, etc. He mentioned that I was essentially accusing you of racism. After the conversations we'd had about your feelings with regard to giving out the book, etc, I can only imagine how fucking hurtful and infuriating this must have been.

Manny, I can't even begin to apologize. I don't know where any of this came from. With Colin's help, I pieced together some of it and all I can say is that I can't explain it, I really truly and honestly can't. Before Colin pulled me aside to talk tonight, I had no idea that I had been such an asshole, I sensed something very strange in the air, but I didn't realize the extent of it. There is something about being incredibly drunk on tequila which in more recent times has made me behave in increasingly erratic and unexplainable ways. (What to do about that is, of course, a separate issue entirely.) I guess that there's no way to prove that there

227

is absolutely nothing deep in my subconscious that would explain this ridiculous behavior. I can only imagine that in my drunken haze, I thought I was being funny, I don't know.

This is not a case of my simply being embarrassed, as was the case with the Estee baseball thing (Jesus, it's been a good week for me). I am much more obsessed with the fact that I caused you some pain and embarrassment and that I have somehow damaged our relationship. As you said, we'll get past this. I can only hope to earn again the trust that I was proud you had in me. I suck and I'm deeply sorry.

Greg

CHAPTER 92

Ava: There were two couples down there and they were making too much noise, and two male friends. One group was making way too much noise. It was Donald Trump's son. The other guy knocked him on the head with a pint glass.

Noam: Knocked Trump's son?

Ava: Knocked him on the head. So this guy, we called the police, this guy was arrested, but Donald Trump wanted to sue us for improper environment or something. So Manny called him and he said, "I'm a father, I totally understand, I would do the same thing, but maybe I could appeal to you as somebody who understands." So he came from that and then Donald Trump liked him and he said, "Okay, we'll work it out," and he said, "But I need you to publicly apologize." So Manny went on the stage downstairs and it got filmed and it was on some show like *E* or *Entertainment Tonight* and that's what happened.

Steve: I don't remember that.

Noam: I don't remember either.

Steve: It aired?

Ava: Yes, it aired, I think I have video of it somewhere. I'll try to find it. I'll try to find it. So much stuff.

Noam: Andrew's trying to sell a book on the Comedy Cellar.

Ava: So that's what happened. He was very nice with Manny.

Author: He was eventually, but there's like quotes in the paper, because I think Manny said Trump Jr. was being too noisy, and Donald Trump was like, "That doesn't sound like my son, my son's a very quiet boy, it wouldn't have been him."

Noam: Yeah, first my father popped off a little bit and he regretted it. He regretted it.

Ava: Exactly, exactly.

Noam: And then he also said that Donald Trump let him talk and then at some point he said, "Okay Manny, this is how it's going to be," and I remember my father saying he was obviously speaking to a guy who's used to being listened to when he wants to talk.

CHAPTER 91

Joe DeRosa: We didn't sit at the table because Jay didn't work at the club yet, so he didn't sit at the table, which meant I definitely wasn't going to sit at the table but, you know, we sat across from the table and I was amply mocked by Keith and everybody immediately.

Author: How did it feel? You seem someone who's quite able to take it, that kind of, I guess that kind of teasing, but the first time you went in there and you couldn't sit at this table, because only certain people could sit at this table, what did they say to you? Did you retaliate?

Joe: I don't remember exactly ... No, no, I was intimidated, I was very intimidated, because a lot of those guys were guys I had watched on TV and stuff, you know. So to me it might as well have been, like, George Clooney and Brad Pitt or whatever. I was in awe of them because I wanted to be a comic and I knew them as great comics so, but, you know, you kind of laugh because you're being included in some way, but I used to take it really hard. That's the one thing I really appreciated about the Cellar was, like, it really thickened my skin up. Because I'm still a sensitive guy, but, like, I was really sensitive. I would take everything to heart. And then one day Keith was like, "Stupid, we make fun of you because we like you." He's like, "If we didn't like you, we wouldn't talk to you. That's worse. That means nobody knows you're there." I was like, alright, well I'll take that I guess.

CHAPTER 90

Keith Robinson: We're deep into our sessions. Like, you had to watch everything you wear. If you wore the wrong thing, it's on. Like, I wore a pair of sneaks. I lasted one night with them. I wore the wrong jeans with these sneaks and it highlighted how bad these sneaks were, and they got on me so bad, but I knew Kev was after my sneaks so I brought another pair of sneaks and I left them in the trunk of the car. They were getting on me so bad I just ran out, ran to the car, put my safe sneaks on and ran back, because if not, they would have been on at my sneaks all night long. It's not going to happen. I'm the guy that gets people, I don't get got.

CHAPTER 89

DC Benny: It was like, alright already with the fucking *Tough Crowd*. I was happy for everybody, I loved Colin, I'm happy that everybody had a sort of venue to do what they did at the Cellar table. I did not really participate too much in that, just sitting at the Cellar table, you know. I think it was a couple of reasons. I've done a few of these roasts and the last thing you would think ... There are some comedians I've done jokes about that took it really, really hard. And it's just, I was like, I don't know, I'd rather be liked. That's my thing. I'd rather be liked. So, you know, you've got the Cellar table every time you get there, those guys doing their thing. Whatever, you jump in a little bit, jump out a little bit, but at a certain point ... I got there one night and it's going on at the table and it's going on on the TV and it's like, fuck, enough already. Enough already. It's annoying. It was just annoying. It was like, sometimes it's funny, sometimes it's just fucking annoying.

CHAPTER 88

Dov Davidoff: They were like a pack of hyenas, but that were very perceptive and very funny and smart, and so I remember examining my jeans and everything I was wearing before I walked into the club. I went over with a fine-tooth comb to make sure that nothing stood out in such a way that one of those animals would be able to attach themselves to it. But at the same time, I have nothing but respect for Patrice and Colin and Jim and those guys. Colin's a particularly brilliant human being.

CHAPTER 87

Author: You told the studio audience not to applaud on *Tough Crowd*.

Colin: I told the audience every show, don't applaud.

Author: Why?

Colin: I'd say it on the air too. I said, "Don't applaud. Either laugh or don't." Because I felt like it was a pandering thing more than a ... The whole point of comedy is not agreement. It's laughter or not laughter. It's involuntary.

CHAPTER 86

Rich Vos: I just remember me and Patrice attacking Dat Phan on *Tough Crowd*. I watched a clip on YouTube and felt bad years later after watching it, probably recently. I sent him an apology. We were very rough on him.

Author: By email?

Rich: No, by homing fucking pigeon. Yeah, by email. We beat down a guy that wasn't ready to be … That wasn't in our league. It would be like two high-school kids beating up a middle schooler or whatever and after I saw the video years later it was an ambush and it wasn't … I just felt bad. So I sent him an email and I said, "I hope everything's going well for you."

CHAPTER 85

Colin: What I remember, you know, is going downstairs to the Cellar, watching guys on stage all talking about, being brutally honest about race, about ethnicity, how they felt about political correctness. There's just no political correctness. Political correctness is just the death of comedy. It's just unbelievable. So that was basically what happened. But downstairs I'd see the antidote for what I saw as this whole society of platitudes and false empathy, and this kind of fake compassion, and so when I got a chance to do this show, that's what I brought. I brought all these people and I was like, let's try to make it like the Comedy Cellar. The table and the stage, you know. It wasn't just about the table. The whole show's point was not just for people to insult each other, it was also to talk honestly and brutally about society. And the beauty of it was, when somebody got too big on their platform everybody would try to trash your clothes or your outfit, or if I tried to organize things too well they trashed me, so it was kind of … That was the subplot. I felt like the trashing of each other was the subplot of *Tough Crowd*. I felt like *Tough Crowd* was about the honesty of talking about how you felt about ethnicity and all these different things.

CHAPTER 84

Colin: Where I grew up was very multi-racial and very open as far as the way people spoke to each other. You know what I mean? If you were funny, you said whatever you wanted and that was it. And even if you weren't funny there was a culture of what other people just call breaking balls, or other people call being sarcastic. But anyway, at the start there just seemed to be different people that you could always joke with. Any comedian. Comedians are good like that, but then at the Cellar it became, somewhere along the line, it was just certain people starting to hang out there at the table that were more enthusiastic about it than others. It became like a sport. You'd bust balls and the rules were, you can't cry if it gets a little brutal, everyone else will regulate it. You know what I mean? Nobody can really take offense that badly.

CHAPTER 83

Noam: I don't think he was upset about the petition.

Author: You don't think so? Ted Alexandro didn't think he was, he thought he was fine with it. The only person who said he did think your dad was upset was Mitch Fatel. He said he was sitting at the table one time and your dad was upset when he looked through this petition, and he was upset that all these comedians had signed it, and Mitch hadn't signed this petition, so your dad was happy with Mitch.

Noam: Okay. The word "upset" is not very precise. Certainly you get a petition and a bunch of comedians sign it, it's upsetting. But I took you to mean that my father thought that they had done something they should not have done or had no right to do. No. I don't think he was upset with them. He wasn't angry with them. He might have been upset that he thought it wasn't fair, but I can tell you this, it wasn't a big thing. I would remember. I had my father's ear. And he didn't think along those terms anyway. He would have just looked at it … He never begrudged people making money. He always liked to pay the most. There is always the case that people tend to overestimate how much money the boss is making. I mean, I do it. I go into a place and see it's crowded and say to myself, "Oh my god, this guy must be making a fortune." And I stop and go, "What the fuck's the matter with me, don't I know better?"

CHAPTER 82

Manny reads Ted's petition,

New York City is the Mecca of stand-up comedy and we, as comedians, are proud to share that tradition with you, the clubs providing comedians with a venue to perform. However, while the clubs are thriving we feel that we are not being adequately compensated for our work. The weekend rates for comedians have seen a negligible increase in the past fifteen to twenty years, and in some cases no increase at all. Again, New York City is the standard and with this in mind we ask that our weekend pay be adjusted to a level commensurate with the revenue being generated and the work that we do. The last pay increase of any note for comedians was in the mid-eighties. Based on cost of living increases, $50 in 1987 being equivalent to $100 in 2002, we, the undersigned, ask that our pay for weekend (Friday and Saturday night) spots be increased to $100 per set. It is our intention to work together in a spirit of collaboration, mindful that we are part of a great tradition and hopeful that we can continue to contribute to and honor that tradition. Please feel free to contact us through the below email address, or through one of the phone numbers below, to discuss this matter further. Thank you for your time.

Sincerely,

NYcomics@aol.com

TED ALEXANDRO ___-___-____

EDDIE BRILL ___-___-____

WILLIAM STEPHENSON ___-___-____

VIC HENLEY ___-___-____

GREG GIRALDO

TODD BARRY

JEFF ROSS

JIM GAFFIGAN

LEWIS BLACK

NICK DI PAOLO

SUSIE ESSMAN

JUDY GOLD

MARC MARON

VANESSA HOLLINGSHEAD

WALI COLLINS

TOM PAPA

CYNTHIA KOURY

RICH VOS

KEITH ROBINSON

JOE VEGA

SHERROD SMALL

TONY ROCK

JIM FLORENTINE

RUSS MENEVE

PETE CORREALE

BEN BAILEY

DC BENNY

PATRICE O'NEAL

JIM DAVID

KEVIN BRENNAN

FRANK GIA

KEVIN FLYNN

RICH FRANCESE

GREG CAREY

AL DUCHARME

VINNIE BRAND

CORY KAHANEY

TOM COTTER

JUDAH FRIEDLANDER

MODI

JOHNNY LAMPERT

JUSTIN McKINNEY

TIM YOUNG

KYLE DUNNIGAN

JOE MATARESE

BILLY BURR

ANDRE FERNANDEZ

GREG FITZSIMMONS

MIKE BIRBIGLIA

SPANKY

ERIC McMAHON

BUDDY FITZPATRICK

ROD REYES

BRAD TRACKMAN

JORDAN RUBIN

TOM SHILLUE

PAUL MECURIO

ROSS BENNETT

GODFREY

LOUIS CK

SARAH SILVERMAN

ANDREW KENNEDY

BILL McCARTY

DAVE ATTELL

MIKE DENICOLA

JIM NORTON

TODD ALLEN LYNN

TRACY MORGAN

HOOD

JR HAVLAN

JIMM D

SAM GREENFIELD

ROB MAGNOTTI

GARY GREENBERG

KAREN BERGREEN

LENNY MARCUS

JOHN PRIEST

ROBERT KELLY

STEVE BYRNE

MOODY McCARTHY

BERNADETTE PAULEY

SUNDA CROONQUIST

CHAPTER 81

Hood Qaim-Maqami stops doing the suicide bomber joke,

I dropped it ... except for one time when Manny very kindly suggested that I re-try it at the Cellar. I did and immediately got heckled with a very loud, "That's not funny!" Oddly enough, the heckle was a perfect lead-in to the follow-on plane/Israel jokes. But it didn't feel right. I'm confident that Manny would have supported my continuing to use it. But for me, it wasn't about having the courage or being comfortable with the cringe. It also wasn't about the thin-skinned PC types who would heckle without having been directly impacted. In fact, I was more directly impacted by 9/11 than ninety-nine per cent of Americans and New Yorkers. But that's still not one hundred per cent. And for me, it was about avoiding that rare instance when someone more directly impacted, someone who had lost a loved one, was actually in the crowd. Others might look at it as an opportunity to be New York edgy. I think it's just callous.

CHAPTER 80

Hood: I met Robin Williams. He was sitting in the back of the Cellar, maybe a couple of days after 9/11. And I walked in to do my set. He was sitting in the back talking with Manny and others. And again, I had never until that point met Robin Williams. When I came to the back they were all sitting and Manny goes, "This is Hood. This is the guy I told you about," to Robin Williams. And Robin said something like, "Are you still doing the bomb bit?" And I said, "Yeah. Why? Did something happen?"

CHAPTER 79

Days earlier, Hood's running late for work. He's about ten blocks away when a plane flies into his office.

His spot at the Cellar tonight is canceled. The club's closed.

The next day, Ava opens the Olive Tree again.

Ava: I live upstairs so I came down here and opened up.

Noam: We couldn't get deliveries though.

Ava: I went to 14th Street and I got them from there with the shopping cart.

Noam: I remember the first day was easier, and then the couple of days later it became harder and they wouldn't let people down, but they would let the vendors come down to deliver.

Ava: I called Manny. Manny was … He couldn't get here because of the trains and he was like, "Whatever you want to do." And I remember, it sounds corny to say, but I had just been talking to my sister who lives in Israel and I'd said, "How do you keep going about your business? How do you survive with children?" And she said, "The trick is just to keep like the same as normal. Just keep it as normal." And for some reason that came into my head.

The Cellar opens again after three days.

CHAPTER 78

Author: People are making assumptions about you when they look at you.

Hood: And it played off all those assumptions Andrew. I wasn't a … Most of the terrorism that was happening, even pre-9/11, it's not really Iranian, and on top of that, I'm not a Muslim, but not only does it not matter on stage, it also … All joking aside, I do get flagged for random searches more often than maybe random signifies. Right? So it's not just onstage that I get tagged as a potential threat, it's everywhere, and as soon as I start talking people realize I'm not a terrorist threat, but even as a light-skinned Middle Eastern person, there's still enough Middle Eastern in my look that …

Author: That was the whole joke to me, or that was part of the joke to me, was that you were getting up on stage and making people think about the way they think about someone who looks like you. It seemed brilliant to me.

Hood: But Andrew, even when I did the bomb thing, you have to realize, I didn't do things like speak in a thick accent. I spoke exactly as I'm talking to you. And if you haven't heard the joke, you've read about it, it would be … I'd get on stage, I'd thank everyone for coming, I'd tell them I'm originally from Iran. That inevitably, when you say you're from anywhere you get some kind of applause, but it would usually get no applause. At which point I said, "Thank you, I feel the warmth," which would get a laugh. But then I say, "Well, if you're going to be that kind of a crowd, I'd like to start off tonight by doing something in the name of Allah." I would lift my shirt, show the bomb. That's when, pre-9/11, the crowd would just explode with laughter. And then I'd go, "Wow, thank God you reacted that way. Not all crowds get this kind of humor. I did this joke two weeks ago in Israel and cleared off the entire plane." Right, so you can see how pre-9/11 … And Manny, when he first saw me do this, getting back to the Comedy Cellar, Manny was … God, I really miss him. I'm not exaggerating when I say I loved Manny. I really loved Manny. But he would see it, and he was deeply conservative in the opinions he had, but he was also a humanist.

CHAPTER 77

Author: Can you remember any other incidents like that, where it's got into the public domain that there's been a problem at the club?

Noam: Yeah, there was a big Seinfeld …

Ava: Yes, Maija.

Noam: Maija. What was her last name?

Steve: I didn't know her. She made the movie.

Noam: She wanted to videotape her own act and then they started … They couldn't record when Seinfeld was on stage, but they did record for her documentary or something like that, and then they got into a fight with Seinfeld about it.

Ava: In the hallway, right.

Noam: In the hallway, and then, oh, he was going to have his thugs come down and take care of my father, and my father ran upstairs, and somehow the media got wind of it and it was in the *Post*.

Ava: Absolutely. Actually, he remembered it exactly right.

Author: So what happened in that situation? I didn't quite understand. So she was filming. She wasn't supposed to film Seinfeld but she did?

Noam: She had her boyfriend with her. He was a tough guy. He did end up having words with Seinfeld.

Author: In the Cellar?

Noam: Now you have to understand that Seinfeld was really one of our first entrees into the big time in terms of a huge star coming regularly … Before that people who'd started here had become famous, but he was one of the first really famous guys who started coming down here regularly, filming his documentary here, and it was important. The idea that he might have been turned away or discouraged from coming back, or feel uncomfortable here, this was huge. It was a knife to our throats.

CHAPTER 76

Christian Charles: As far as, you know, these guys walking into those clubs, this is the oxygen of these places. When Jerry Seinfeld walks into your club or Dave Chappelle walks in or Robin Williams walks in because they want to work out, that's everything to these guys, so that relationship is really straightforward.

CHAPTER 75

Author: You were filming half the time and Gary Streiner was filming half the time?

Christian: Yeah. This is really ... This to me is the essence of why this film ... There's a bunch of reasons I think it works. I had his trust. And I'm not sure he would like me saying this, but I think he used Gary and I as a crutch. Because he was quietly terrified about going into clubs by himself. And we were a little bit of a buffer for him. Because it allowed him to just have his buddies with him and kind of defend himself from a little bit of the need to directly engage with the community. But the most important thing about this film and its success to me is I had the most famous man in America and I had to present him in a way that people would accept him as a regular guy. Meanwhile he's flying around in private jets, he's worth, you know, $400 million and he's got houses all over the place and the biggest collection of Porsches on the planet and it's not an easy task. And so we made the decision that we would shoot with these prosumer cameras and look like a couple of bozos, and never really kind of present ourselves as a flashy professional operation. So Gary and I made that decision very early on. So we shot it ourselves. At one point I clipped a wireless mic to Jerry, early on in the process, and he said, "This is not a film, this is my life." And he actually got quite frustrated that night with the fact that he was wired.

Author: Where was that?

Christian: I think that was ... Oh goodness I want to say it was the Cellar. And you've been there, you know, this is not a place of polish. This is like ... This is like, you know, it's the most organic thing a building can be.

Author: So you think in the Cellar or in the Olive Tree above it you were clipping a mic to him and he objected to it, he said, "This is my life." And did you take it off him?

Christian: He wore it once and he never wore it again. Yeah, he went up on stage with it and he just wasn't happy. He wasn't happy. So that was ...

Author: I was just going to say, you named a kind of camera?

Christian: Prosumer. As in it's a professional consumer camera. It was the Sony TRV 900. It was shot on mini-digital video tape and the footage was ... We were very, very lucky. We had this genius who made the film look like 16mm. We tested multiple conversions and this guy's version of it was like fifteen times better than anyone else and it kind of saved us.

Author: And some of the critics were unhappy with how the film looked.

Christian: Fuck them.

Author: I wondered if Jerry ever said anything about that. Did he ever see any of the footage and say, "Why aren't you using ..."

Christian: Oh yeah, he was very much involved, and I think that's the point of it. They kind of missed the point of it. Sound was tricky. We actually ended up with Frank Morrone, who is like this multi-award-winning mixer, to mix it because we had to dig, dig, dig to get the sound to be ... But the point of it is that it looks that way very deliberately because you see Jerry as a real human being. You're seeing all these guys as real human beings.

CHAPTER 74

Colin: That was before 9/11, I think it's important people realize that, and Jerry had just come back to New York, and when I saw Hassan, I go, "Hassan, if you kill him you'll be a fucking hero in all the Arab lands for eternity." I didn't know about the seventy-two virgins in those days. It was before 9/11. I go, "You'll be a hero, that's the king of the Jews right there."

CHAPTER 73

Hatem Gabr: Have you heard of Hassan? He was a manager there, one of the biggest managers, an Egyptian guy. I can't believe you've never heard of him.

CHAPTER 72

Noam: You've got to speak to Ava and Hassan. You're really not going to do the book right if you don't speak to Ava and Hassan.

CHAPTER 71

Hassan Ragheb: When any famous comedian came to the Olive Tree, Manny used to respect him and to give him like a big, big ... To make him feel like a very big man, you know what I mean? To make a lot of things special for him. So one time Jerry Seinfeld came and he parked his car in front of the Olive Tree.

Author: His Porsche? Was it a Porsche?

Hassan: Porsche, yeah. And he said to me, "Take the key and put it in Manny's park." So I looked to him and I said, "What you talking about? Who are you? You tell me about your car, why?" When Manny came of course he screamed at me. I said, "Manny, I don't know him and he asked me to park his car. I'm not here to park people's cars."

Author: So Jerry Seinfeld parked in front of the Olive Tree, got out of his car, took his key out, gave you the key and said ...

Hassan: To watch his car.

Author: To move it if somebody came along basically?

Hassan: So anyway, after that we had a lot of talk and especially Manny tells me always who's this and who is famous, so when he came I treat him very, very nice.

CHAPTER 70

Colin: I mean, once again, if you spoke to the wait staff, they'd have a whole different story maybe.

Author: Because he was a tough boss?

Colin: Because he was a tough boss. Like, he saw everything that was happening. So he'd be talking about Israel or whatever and he'd go, "Why is that still happening?" You know what I mean? He'd sit there, but he'd be watching here.

CHAPTER 69

Hatem Gabr: So we have this table called twenty-one, that's the table for the comedians. And then there's table twenty-three, which is next to it. So these are the comedians that are at the Comedy Cellar but they don't dare to sit at twenty-one, but they want to listen, so they will sit there. And then you have two other tables. Comedians that want to be there, but they're not performing, and comedians that will never perform there. They're just there. So you already have three audiences, and the funny part is, we never told anybody where to sit. They know. Like, "I will never perform here, I'm just going to go sit there." They know their table. So if you get called to the back table, it's like you're getting called to the witness stand, like in a trial. "Holy shit, I am going to be grilled." Because you don't want to be there. So if they say, like, "Manny wants you at table twenty-one …" If he wants me at table twenty-three, that's a different story, but twenty-one is a problem. This means that I'm going to be attacked. So when you go there you will have Louis CK. You can have Colin Quinn. You can have Nick Di Paolo. Tom Papa. Some of the funniest people on the stage. Greg Giraldo of course. You will have Jim Norton. So you go there, they're probably debating about something and they're going to ask you the question, and you'd better answer right, because, you know, that probably … That means there's two lines. For example, I don't want to be against Jim Norton, because he's going to just destroy you. So, whatever. So that's one. Now, in this particular table you will, you know … A comedian will go back and forth. One time a comedian called Tony Daro, he's one of the great debaters and he's always against Manny and Israel and all that. So one time he had a huge fight with Manny at table twenty-one and they decided to settle it as a debate. So they had literally a big table in the middle of the Olive Tree, about maybe forty people, comedians, and they all show up with their documents and stuff and start debating each other. But the funny part is, customers walking in, they have no idea. The whole middle section became a debate. One sitting on one end and Manny on the other end, all books and stuff. And in the middle, twenty comedians each side, screaming at each other.

CHAPTER 68

Lenny Marcus: Dean Obeidallah and Manny would yell at each other for hours over Israel and … But I hate politics. I hate politics. If I brought up sports, even to this day if I bring up sports at the table Noam gets really mad, like, whatever. I can't even sit down. I can't do it. It was horrible. I hated watching them talk about politics. Rich Vos talking about the Middle East? I mean, come on man.

CHAPTER 67

Noam: I'm walking towards Sixth Avenue and I walked by a homeless guy at some point, and I don't remember ... I just remember noticing him. He looked at me and then I keep walking, I guess this is before the garage, and I'm walking towards the garage and a homeless guy walks past me. He's walking faster and he catches up with a cop, and I see him talking to the cop, and then he points at me, and then the cop comes over to me and he says, "Up against the wall." And like, "What?" And he very roughly puts me up against the wall, and I try to explain to him who I was. I say, "Listen, I own the Olive Tree." The cops all eat at the Olive Tree. The Olive Tree has been there for twenty-five years at that point, so every Sixth Precinct cop knows the Olive Tree. I pointed at the Fat Black Pussycat, "And I own this place." And he grabbed me and goes, "Shut up." Like that. And he was rough with me, and he frisks me and blah blah blah.

Author: What does that mean? Hands up against the wall and kicks your legs apart?

Noam: Like in the movies?

Author: And then feels you all over, as in, between your legs as well, to check you don't have a gun or something?

Noam: Yeah. I mean, I don't remember being molested or anything, but yeah.

Author: But pats down the outside of your leg and pats down the inside of your leg?

Noam: Yeah. At some point he said he was checking me for a gun because the guy said that. And I remember trying to tell him, you know, "That guy's a homeless guy." I couldn't understand it. So it was a very unpleasant experience, but I knew a city councilman at the time who I was friends with and I told him the story and he, who was also a lawyer, was pretty outraged because apparently the cop had not followed any proper procedure. There was no probable cause. I don't know what the rules are. So the cop was, I think, reprimanded in some way.

Author: And did you get a ticket? How did you know who the cop was?

Noam: No, I didn't get a ticket. There's only so many cops in the precinct. I think I knew his name. I think I knew his name. I remember what he looks like.

Author: So he put you against the wall, frisked you, and then said … He was a bit menacing in the way he talked? And then just said, "Okay, free to go"?

Noam: Yeah, and then probably said, "Free to go." And it happened to me two times. The second time wasn't as rough, but the cop threw me up against the wall by the Cafe Wha and I said, "What are you doing?" He says for peeing on the street. I'm like, "Peeing on the street?" And again, I had trouble … He was cutting me off and I said, "Dude, I own this place." Like, "This is my place. Why would I be peeing on the street?" And again, you have to wonder what they were doing. Were they just looking to bust balls? It was bizarre. Or maybe you see a whole big crowd, you think I was the one peeing on the street. I have no idea.

Author: On the first occasion, when was that?

Noam: This is both around 2000 I'd say. Both incidents happened within a pretty short time of each other.

Author: And were the police officers white or black? What was their race?

Noam: The guy who was rough with me was white. The peeing on the street one, I don't remember.

CHAPTER 66

Godfrey: It was one thing I loved about Manny, it was like, we argued about shit all the time.

Author: Like about what?

Godfrey: Oh, politics. Race. The business. Yeah. It was great.

Author: And can you think of an example of something that he argued about?

Godfrey: We would argue about … Sometimes I would argue about the unfairness of black comics and white comics. Sometimes.

Author: What is the unfairness?

Godfrey: You don't know the unfairness? You as a white man do not know the unfairness? Are you just being a journalist?

Author: No, no, I really want to know. That's what I'm trying to figure out.

Godfrey: Oh, I just always think it's just easier for white comedians because they're white. That's it. They're just white.

Author: And what would Manny say?

Godfrey: Manny would be like, "No, that's not true." I was like, "Yes it is, it's very true."

Author: Like, easier to get spots?

Godfrey: No, just in business. White males, it's run by them, so they get more shit. Like, black comics have to be super, super, super-duper funny, funny, funny. A white comic can be okay and still get ten sitcoms and shit. But if you're a person of color you've got to be like super, super extra … And black comics, we day in, day out kill. Murder, murder, murder. And then every once in a while you have a black person that becomes the famous person and then all of a sudden we all have to aspire to be that particular person. We can't just be a whole bunch of different black people. White people, there's nine-hundred white comics that have their own shows. And black comics, there's that one famous black person. Because we always used to call it one negro at a time.

CHAPTER 65

Author: So you were standing outside Mamoun's?

Sherrod Small: Between Mamoun's and the Cellar right there, and I had just finished.

Author: You'd been smoking a spliff, like a cigarette with weed in it?

Sherrod: Yes.

Author: Just finished, stubbed it out or whatever, and the policeman came along?

Sherrod: He came up from Minetta Lane.

Author: And then Manny noticed the policeman talking to you so he came out?

Sherrod: Yep. And then he asked, "What's going on?" They were taking my ID. They were looking at my ID. And Manny was like, "Is there a problem?" And they were like, "Step back." He was like, "This is my property." Now we were standing right in front of the Cellar. He's like, "This is my property. I don't have to step anywhere. You don't have to yell at me. Why are you yelling? What are you, the Gestapo?"

CHAPTER 64

Author: I couldn't quite figure out what the argument was about. And was it on the stairs outside the Cellar when he pushed you?

Allan Havey: It was in the club. And he was pushing me, and Estee said to him, "Leave him alone." I don't know what happened. I really don't know. It goes to show you, it was really important at the time. And it surprised me. I think it was this anger building up. I think too they expected me to be a bigger star and I don't ... I think, and this is what happens, like, people, when I was younger, "Oh, you're going to be this and do that." And I had great success. I had the talk show, did a couple of HBO specials, but it's not enough. It's never enough. You have to always do more. And I think they were disappointed that I wasn't a bigger star than I was.

Author: Really?

Allan: That's just personal. That's what I think personally. You don't have to put that in the book, but I think that's ...

Author: Do you still have the letter that he sent you apologizing?

Allan: I have it. It's tucked away somewhere. It's very gracious. Very simple.

Author: Do you think there'd be any chance of me seeing that?

Allan: No, it's tucked away. I'm sorry.

Author: That's alright, don't worry, it's a lot to ask. Some of the stuff people are letting me see I'm surprised about. But if ever you changed your mind, I'd love to see it.

Allan: If I run across it, you know, I'll kind of look for it, but I know it's tucked away. I didn't throw it away, but it's certainly not something I would show anyone. I showed it to my girlfriend at the time, now my wife. You know, it meant a lot when I got the letter and I wrote back and then I called him. I said, "Did you get the letter?" "Yeah." I said, "Good, because my girlfriend mailed it." He goes, "Oh, you had to have your girlfriend mail it?" So we kind of laughed and got into it. Manny and I could have the biggest argument in the world. I love the guy.

CHAPTER 63

Sherrod: Everybody would see him leave and he'd come out, get in the car, "Bye everybody," drive off. I'm like, "Watch. Two minutes, this motherfucker will drive back around." He would go around the block and come back around, and then any staff he caught out there smoking or taking a break when they weren't supposed to, he would chastise them.

Author: Would he get out of the car and do it?

Sherrod: Yeah, sometimes he would get out the car. Sometimes he would yell out the car. Sometimes they would peek and see the car coming and run back in. It was classic.

Author: Going down MacDougal?

Sherrod: He would go up Minetta or he might drive down to Bleecker and go around that way. He would go around the whole block just to come back around slowly, driving like he was about to do a drive-by. I would say, "Manny, why you so hard on the staff?" He was like, "If you give them an inch they'll destroy the place." But that's his baby. That place, the Olive Tree and the Comedy Cellar, that's his babies man, that shit's everything to him.

CHAPTER 62

Nick Di Paolo: I had a set the next night after I moved back to New York. I had a couple of sets at the Comedy Cellar and I remember going down there, and I had performed there previously many times. And I found myself standing amongst the people at the bar, the customers, and I said to Manny ... Manny came in, who I adore to this day, my favorite personality that I ever met in this business, and I go, "Manny, for Christ's sake, can't we just like reserve that table in the back for the comedians?"

Author: So it was that specific?

Nick: Yeah, oh yeah. I pointed right to the table and he just he gave me, like, a smirk and just, like, a nod, and I don't remember, but I came in the next night ... This was the type of guy he was. I come in the next night and there's the table and it's got a reserved for comedians sign on it, and so I sat right down, proud. But that's the type of guy Manny was, you know. He always put the artist first. There were many nights that I got out of hand on stage and most club owners would have said, "Look, don't come back for a little while." He always defended my political incorrectness. He was a musician himself. He's kind of famous. So he put the artist first, you know.

CHAPTER 61

Ava: Everything was always breaking and I was doing most of the hiring, so desperately needed a carpenter. And not good people were coming in. And John came in. He was a pretty scary-looking guy. Huge guy. Tattoos all over. Long braid. A real character. He had a like a Swastika … An SS tattoo.

Author: He had a Swastika?

Ava: I'm sorry, no, no, no, it was an SS tattoo.

Author: So, like, an SS tattoo. As in, like, the letters SS?

Ava: Yeah, but you know, the Nazi SS. Yeah, and he had a nurse with a …

Author: Was he a former neo-Nazi?

Ava: No, not at all. Not at all. Don't get the wrong idea. Not at all. Not at all. Not at all. He just had these scary tattoos. He had a nurse with a hypodermic needle. He had, like, really bizarre tattoos.

Author: Where was the SS tattoo?

Ava: I saw it, but it was funny, maybe he was wearing shorts. He had a lot on his legs or something. It was small. It was faded. But of course … I know this, but you know, I think … That's when the two lightning bolts are together? Right?

Author: Yeah.

Ava: Like I said, he was a huge guy. Looked like a giant bear, and had this long braid, and anyway, but I interviewed everybody. Don't judge a book by its cover. And I remember he said the things that he could do, I was like, wow, he could do everything, this guy can do everything, electrical plumbing, sheet rock, according to what he said, carpentry, and the stories he was telling me. So I was like, "Okay, it's too good to be true." So I called Noam's carpenter in the Wha, so he came up and interviewed him for me, because he knew if the things … He kind of tested him if that makes sense, because he could do the same things. So he passed that with flying colors and he was like, "Yeah, he looks scary, but, yeah you know, whatever." And I was like, "Alright, I'm going to go ask Manny for a third opinion." So then Manny interviewed him, because I didn't want the responsibility with that SS thing. So Manny interviewed him and he was like, "Yeah, he's really nice. He seems good. So whatever, try it if you want to." Then Manny went and asked … So he said, "Okay, we'll get back to you." So Manny asked Taweel, I think it was Taweel, to ask one of the policemen, because in those days it was neighborhood policemen. He asked one of the neighborhood policemen if he could check him out, as we had his information, and yes, we found out that he was … Well, he had told me this in the interview, that he was from the Hell's Angels, that's why he looked the way he looked, and he said to me, "Don't be scared about the way I look. I was with the Hell's Angels. I'm not with them anymore." And that's why he had that tattoo, because of the Hell's Angels. And so he actually said that to me. He said, "Don't go by what I look like." So they confirmed he had been in the Hell's Angels and had been arrested because of them for armed robbery, he was a bad guy, you know, before he went to prison. And I remember … You know the stairs down to the Comedy Cellar?

Author: Outside?

Ava: From the inside. I don't know, I have this memory, but there was a juke box there at the time. I know you haven't seen a juke box, but there was a juke box in the entrance to the Comedy Cellar. Manny, John and I went to the top of the stairs and I remember Manny saying, "Listen, I know about your background. I'm not going to tell anybody. I checked you out with the police, but I'm going to give you a chance. But they know who you are. And they know what you've done. So if anything happens here, they know who you are." And John was in shock that he got hired. In shock.

CHAPTER 60

Keith: We started our table right around here. You know, a nice rowdy table. Me, Jim Norton. Wherever we were, it was like a table, me, Rich Vos, Jim Norton, Patrice O'Neal. That was it. A certain crew. We come here and play chess and all that. And we see Ray Romano and them back there, quiet, talking about who got Leno. And we set up here and just played chess and fucking screamed at each other, and talked about shoes, shirts and all that shit.

Author: And did Manny hang around with you guys?

Keith: No, why would he? We were just trash really.

Author: So he was up there with Ray Romano.

Keith: He was back there with Ray, Colin, maybe Jon Stewart and all them, but we were here creating a ruckus. We would always play chess, you know, get the chess board out. I scream at Norton. I tease Norton a little bit.

Author: What would you tease him about?

Keith: Lift his pieces up. That prison shit. Like, "Look at you." I lift his queen up, "What kind of panties she got on? Oh, she got good panties." And he'd get mad, "Come on man, don't touch my pieces." "She got real good panties."

Author: So, childish stuff.

Keith: Of course, why not?

CHAPTER 59

The author emails Dan Naturman to ask about Lewis Schaffer. Dan replies,

Lewis stood in front of the club and harassed passersby telling them to come in and see the show. What's interesting is they never asked him to do it. He was MC'ing and did it on his own initiative. He was so good at it that he became the full-time MC for a while.

CHAPTER 58

The author emails Noam,

You said on a podcast once that Lewis Schaffer is a "Comedy Cellar legend, a man in many ways responsible for the modern iteration of the Comedy Cellar." I wondered why that was?

Noam replies,

I really don't know what I've gotten myself into here.

CHAPTER 57

Author: Do you remember the date when you first left the Cellar and went to work at the Boston?

Lewis Schaffer: I don't remember.

Author: The year? Do you remember the year?

Lewis: '96? '97? How do people remember this shit?

Author: I guess if something important happened in your life at the same time.

Lewis: Yeah.

Author: So you went to work at the Boston. Do you remember how Manny reacted?

Lewis: I'd been fired. He got somebody to take my ... I don't know how I told him. He was angry. He was mad at me, but he was also, I think by that point, a bit fed up with me. I mean people don't like me. They don't like me. I think he had thought, "Okay, we'll get somebody else to do it." I remember what happened was, right after ... Well, when I was there the place started to get buzzy on its own. So I was there for a year or two, I don't know how long I was there for, but it was getting buzzy on its own.

Author: The Boston?

Lewis: The Comedy Cellar. It was getting buzzy and Chris Rock had decided to make a return. And so there were, you know, it suddenly became, not suddenly, but it was becoming busier, where it was busy at weekends, and then during the week it was busier. It wasn't dead. So things were alright without me there towards the latter. I mean obviously I made a difference, okay. So I go over to the Boston about a year later and he would drive down West Third Street to get to MacDougal Street, driving in his car, coming from Ardsley or whatever. He'd drive by and every time he saw me outside with my clipboard and he would say, "Lewis, Lewis, look at the car, it's a Lexus." And he'd drive on. He'd say, "Lewis, we've added a third show on a Saturday," and drive by. He'd say, "Lewis, do you know who did a spot at the club last night? Jerry Seinfeld." And he'd drive by. And it's like, the Jews, they do drive-by gloatings. It was about just making me feel bad that his business was doing better than mine.

Author: Did you smile when he did that? Was he smiling when he did that?

Lewis: Yeah, it's Manny. You know what I mean? I wasn't angry at him. Okay. My feeling was, I was thinking what I think all the time, "Why don't people appreciate me? Why didn't he appreciate me?" It was more confused, more confused, but I wasn't angry at Manny, and Manny wasn't angry at me. He was probably a bit relieved, he suddenly had a business again. I mean, he always had a business, it was always going to do well, but suddenly … Yeah.

CHAPTER 56

Lewis: Let me ask you a question. You're a writer. How much of this should I make up?

Author: Don't make any of it up.

Lewis: I don't remember. I just remember I was fired after the meeting.

Author: So the meeting must have happened and then you had this phone call with Manny afterwards, and that's when you yelled at him?

Lewis: I yelled at him. Because I thought he couldn't live without me, but he had a saying, "Everyone's replaceable, including me." Including Manny. He owned the place. He said, "Everyone's replaceable, including me. Don't think you're so special. Everyone's replaceable." And I thought this couldn't be done without me, but I had shown him how to do it, like a schmuck. Not like a schmuck. It was unavoidable.

CHAPTER 55

Lewis: So he calls me and he says, "Lewis, you're annoying people. The show is going on and you're sitting people in the front of the show. The comedian's onstage and you're sitting people." And it was like, I knew you had to sit people ... If you've got five people, they've got to sit in the front row. If they walked in on their own they would sit all the way at the back and not be part of the show, and it wouldn't help attract more people, and it wouldn't be good for the show. So you had to sit them right around the stage. So I would go in and I'd lean over the customer and say, "You have to sit here," when the comedian's on stage, and they did not like that. It was disruptive to them. And they said to me, "You've got to stop," but I knew that if you didn't do that there wouldn't be enough people to create a critical mass to attract other people. This is what I've learned from every single show that I've done since, you've got to get a critical mass. They've got to be sitting there. Even if two people are sitting in the front row laughing, it's better than a hundred people all the way in the back ... I don't know, that's too many for the Cellar. Anyway, thirty people at the back, just leaning against the back wall. So he called me up and said, "You can't do it," and I just started screaming at him.

CHAPTER 54

Lewis: I really thought I was like an amazing person, because suddenly the club got busy, right. And Manny said to Estee that he should make me the five-night-a-week compere, because I was pulling so many people in. And I was very ... I wanted to be in control. I wanted a perfect body. I love that song. And I wanted to be in control and I thought I should be in control, because I know what I'm doing here. Suddenly we have a busy place. I remember Manny, one Tuesday, you know, when it was relatively slow, said to me, "Lewis, I'm thinking of bringing back the Jewish music." Because that's what he used to do with the other place, the Jewish music. "Business is not that good, I'm thinking of bringing back the Jewish music on a Tuesday. What do you think?" That's what Manny would do, he would play with your head.

Author: What did you say?

Lewis: It's Manny, just playing with your head, trying to get you to work harder, trying to get advantage over you, whether he realized it or not, that's what he did.

CHAPTER 53

Lewis: The hardest business in the world is running a club. It's harder than being a comedian. You need total attention. That's what Manny did, he gave everything total attention. He counted up the number of forks and spoons at the end of the night. You know that? Did you know he would do that? He made the staff count up the number of forks and spoons at the end of a shift, at the end of the night, to make sure that nobody was stealing probably.

CHAPTER 52

Author: Lewis said your dad used to get the staff to count the cutlery up at the end of every night.

Noam: Oh, he's so stupid, Lewis.

Author: It might not have been him who said it. I can't remember.

Noam: This is years and years and years ago. There was a time when the waitresses would bus the tables. They would just dump all the dishes. They would dump the silverware into the garbage all the time. So at some point you warn and warn and warn and say, alright, that's it, we're going to have to go into some procedure of accounting. Count up how many forks we have at the beginning of the shift and count out how many we have at the end of the shift to see what's going on. I don't remember that lasting very long. I've had the same kind of … It kind of deteriorated, but I had the same sort of policy for menus at the Fat Black Pussycat. We were just constantly buying new menus. We had expensive menu books and the customers would steal them, and the reason they were able to steal them is after the waitress had taken the order she would neglect to recollect the menu and bring it back. You know normally in a restaurant, after they take your order, the waitress takes the menu back, but our waitresses would … So I got fed up. So I had them text me at the beginning of the shift how many menus they were starting with and text me how many menus they were ending with.

Author: God.

Noam: But you know what? The menus stopped disappearing. They were like $5 a book. They were expensive. So this was not out of any kind of counting pennies. This was just getting ... I mean, there's a better story about this phenomenon. There used to be a policy in the Olive Tree. The drinks of juice were ...

Author: Oh yeah, I got that from you. It's another one I loved.

Noam: So that's what it is. You charge people a quarter, it's not because you want to make the quarter, but all of a sudden they either drink the whole juice or they don't drink it at all. You have to have some way to make an incentive for people to care, especially about something that they consider to be a small change item of negligible value, but actually adds up to significant money throughout an organization. So, like, no glass of orange juice matters, but the entire ...

Author: It's death by a thousand cuts isn't it.

Noam: Yes, that's exactly right. By the way, just to go back, so you know, if there would be any criticism about the way my father was as a businessman it would be exactly the opposite of what that story implies. He was very uninterested and had to work to interest himself in these kind of nickel and dime issues. Margins, costs of goods, all stuff which is exactly the way all the most successful restaurants and bars live and die, that stuff. They know exactly how many ounces of alcohol go into a drink, how much it costs. And he had almost no interest in that whatsoever.

CHAPTER 51

Larry Doyle interviews Manny for a feature for *New York Magazine*. It's about *the bleak state of stand-up* in the city. Larry types up the quotes,

I don't see that kind of caliber now, but maybe when I look back on the people we have today, maybe I'll be more nostalgic.

They copy one another, not only with their material, but how they approach the microphone, how they deliver the punchline.

There are people who might not be as good as other comics, but who are more predictable in terms of pleasing the audience, and that's what's more important to me. I'm constantly having squabbles with the comedians about this, who think of themselves as artists and who think it's more important to work on their art than to be funny.

I want to get a more interactive kind of thing, not maybe like a gong show ...

We all tend to romanticize the past.

CHAPTER 50

Larry interviews Marc Maron for the same feature,

Marc: I'll tell you something about some of the clubs in this city. I mean, they haven't been what they used to be in a long time. The scene isn't what it used to be. And they are very strong personalities, and that's putting it lightly, you know, what they encourage and what they don't. Each club picks their own little stable of people. You know what I mean? And it's all based on that particular club owner's sensibility. Club owners, for the most part, aren't known to be visionaries, you know, and they want to keep asses in seats and they want to sell drinks. So you can pretty much believe that most clubs pander to competence, you know, if not pure fucking hackiness.

CHAPTER 49

Larry interviews Sarah Silverman for the feature,

Sarah: Club owners are going with safe choices. Nobody's being encouraged to be eclectic or to try new things, or see where the crowd leads them.

CHAPTER 48

Larry interviews Louis for the feature,

Louis: The crowds aren't out there right now. I mean, they're not showing up, so it's not … Again, it's a vicious cycle. I don't know how much people can be expected to put in as far as effort if they're not being paid back. And the audiences are not appreciative of lots of good stand-up. But again, we're in this populist kind of field, and the trick is to try to take stuff that's … I think the artistic challenge is to take stuff that's hard for them to grasp and make them laugh at it and grasp it. I mean, it's easy to … Like at Rebar, it's easy to fill a room with people that you know and that all identify with you, and to find people that are like you and make them laugh. That's not hard to do, because they are like you. I think the interesting challenge is to go to places where people don't relate to you, and make them relate to you, you know, without compromising. I think that's really the great thing that can be accomplished, you know. Like, Dave Attell can work any fucking crowd in the world, you know, and that's a great thing to be able to do. It's just that these little rooms that are popping, like Rebar and the ones in LA, where pretty much everybody there is an insider and knows somebody who is performing and agrees with their politics and sort of their cultural background, what are the chances … What, are you gonna bomb? You know. What are the chances that it's not going to go well? It's just silly to me.

CHAPTER 47

Noam writes a letter,

Dear Mr. Mayor,

My name is Noam Dworman. I am the owner and operator of three well known restaurants and nightclubs in Manhattan — The Comedy Cellar, the Olive Tree Cafe, and the Cafe Wha. I am also an attorney, although I do not practice.

I'll be very brief because I'm sure you're too busy to be reading this to begin with. Quite simply, I just want to tell you that I'm a huge supporter of yours. I think an administration which holds your priorities is the only hope for New York City at this very critical time in our history. Additionally, I would like to offer my services to help the city in any way possible. I would be very happy to invite city organizations to use my establishments for meetings, or anything else, free of charge. Also, if there are committees, or panels which need input from New York small business owners on the subjects of restaurants, nightlife, tourism, or other related areas, I would love to participate.

Mr. Giuliani, your election has given me a new sense of optimism about my own future in this city. I think I could provide an intelligent insight into a traditionally important sector of the city's economy, and I am eager to be involved.

Sincerely,

Noam Dworman

PS Please forgive the absence of my signature, because I am sending this letter through CompuServe Email.

CHAPTER 46

Noam: This might have been the last straw, when we stopped bringing money home. He was walking around the corner with money and there was a guy waiting in the garage, and they held him up at gunpoint, took the money. Ava would remember even better than I do. And that was scary because of the gun. And then Ava was also robbed making a bank deposit. That was the worst one of all because she was actually assaulted.

Author: When your dad was held up at gunpoint was that in the Eighties or Nineties?

Noam: It had to be in the Nineties I think. New York was like a jungle in the Nineties. People have no idea and no recollection of how bad it was. It was ridiculous.

Author: That's why these stories are interesting, because as much as I'm trying to do other stuff with the book, it's nice to show the way New York used to be.

Noam: It was just crack addicts all over the place and it was scary as hell. And it's one of, this is probably not for your book, but it's faded in everybody's memories such that people make a lot of the fact that they punished crack much differently than cocaine. You've heard these arguments, right?

Author: Yeah.

Noam: That it's supposed to be racist and all that?

Author: Yeah.

Noam: It couldn't be further from the truth. It's such an inaccurate take on reality. The fact was that crack was a daily threat to people's lives. People just walking down the street and crack addicts were a source of violence. Cocaine was something rich people were doing, you know, in their homes and it wasn't a threat to society. In other words, the crackdown on crack wasn't because they didn't want people taking drugs, although I'm sure that's part of it, it was that it was such a menace to society. It was making the city unliveable.

CHAPTER 45

Lewis: The place was absolutely dead, and there were times when Hassan, the manager, would demand, or ask, or try to ask, in his nice way, for the comedians to sit in the audience to make it look like there were people there. Okay? There were like none. Not a single person coming in. And of course they wouldn't do it, because they weren't quite used to the idea that the bottom had fallen out of the market.

CHAPTER 44

Gregg Rogell: There was one night when there was only one guy in the audience. He was from Holland and spoke broken English. And I remember I was going on first and Manny said, "We're having a show." So I sat down at the table with the guy and chatted with him for twenty minutes. That was my spot.

CHAPTER 43

Mike Royce: Weeknights, you weren't even sure if they were going to have a show. A few times we actually didn't have a show, because there was no audience. And quite frequently I would have to start the show with, like, four people in the audience. And you know, it's a showcase, so people come in and out during the night, but I mean, I would emcee and there were four people sitting there. I did do a little banter, you know, with the four people, and you see a couple stick their head in the door and then I'd be like, "Come in." And they'd come in and then they'd sort of realize there are only four people there and, shit, I'd have to pitch all of them into staying, "There's more people in the show, we're just starting, blah, blah, blah." And this happened night after night for a couple of years with not too many exceptions. And on more than one occasion I had to literally start the show with no audience and then I'm just on stage and there's no one in the audience, but the reason is so that when people come through the door and the show has started, they think there's a show going on, and from the stage I beg them to stay.

CHAPTER 42

Catch A Rising Star closes.

The Improv closes.

Who's on First closes.

Comedy U closes.

Manny asks some staff to take a temporary wage cut. After about six weeks Ava makes the money back up to them. The Cellar stays open.

Louis: There was no one going to see stand-up anymore. And at the Cellar there would literally sometimes be no audience and Manny would make you go on stage anyway to literally perform for no people, because the thinking was, and it was proper, was that if somebody is curious on the street and they stick their head in and there's nothing going on … You've got to prime the pump, something has to be happening, so it was horrible and humiliating to do these sets, but of course they were formative. It was a great experience. And also Manny was trying to keep the place going, he was trying to keep the place going for all of us, but at the time he would have these meetings to talk about what can we do about this new crisis of comedy falling apart, and there I don't think that was his best … Like, he would just criticize everybody, and he and I used to fight a lot, so I just didn't want to be part of it. I just knew that I would not do well in those meetings, and I had started getting less and less work at the Cellar and I was getting a little bit bitter about it, and so I went to the meeting to meet another comedian to leave and Manny saw me in the door and he said, "Hey, why don't you come in here, you have opinions, let's hear your goddamn opinions." He said it kind of combatively and I said, "I'm not coming into this meeting Manny because you're mean. You're a mean person. I don't like the way you talk to comedians. I don't like you." And I pointed at Estee and I said, "And you're mean and I just don't want any part. I don't care if you use me or not." And Manny said, "Not only are you stupid, you're not funny." And everybody went, "Whoa." And Manny said, "Hey, he called me mean." And I learned something about him there, which is that he didn't think I'm stupid and unfunny, it's just that I hit him, I fucking insulted him, so he insulted me back. I never got upset anymore when Manny would say something mean because I knew he was just fucking … He was a fighter. So it didn't bother me.

Author: How did Estee take it when you called her mean?

Louis: She started to say something and he stopped her. He didn't let … Because he wanted to take the lead in the fight. I left. I didn't work at the Cellar for years.

CHAPTER 41

Juanita Dworman: Manny would come in and walk across the room and say, "That light is out, fix this, clean that table." And he was friendly. He spoke with everybody. It was more of a social thing to come down.

Author: You were a waitress then. What happened when it was quiet?

Juanita: Well, if the Cellar wasn't busy he'd have the waitresses sit and be the audience. He'd say, "Take off your aprons, sit down."

CHAPTER 40

Louis: There was a big fucking, what do you call it, gyro thing out front. Yeah, and it was at the front out on the street, and Hassan ran that and would serve this Middle Eastern food. And at the time when the war was going on Manny had turned the big screen into a TV to show the war, and I remember that all of the Arab cooks and workers and Hassan were all sitting watching, and they were huddled together, and Hassan was asking me for interpretation because it was going by too fast, the talking, so he would say, "Can you explain to us what's happening?" And I realized that these people were all from this fucking region, this was their home, and they were worried. And it struck me, because Manny employed all these guys and he had this little microcosm of the Middle East that he brought to this place, and he brought so much tradition, coming over from Israel as an immigrant, and being a folk musician and creating a place for folk musicians to play and then getting these strange instruments and he had stand-up, and how he just protected the values of that place, of his customers having a good time, and his comedians having a place to work, and keeping it all afloat during tough times, instead of just bailing. I admired him tremendously for that. And anyway, one time Noam was telling a story about how he had been to the Middle East, this was during the Gulf War, and they were talking about how much everybody hated Israel and all this stuff, and he said, you know, Noam said, "I've traveled all over the Middle East." He had traveled in every Arab country, and he said, "Known to be a Jew. I would be taken in. Everywhere, taken into people's homes. They would feed

me and take care of me and treat me like family everywhere I went."
And I said, "Why do you think that isn't extrapolated? Why then do
these countries hate Israel so much?" And Manny said, very joyfully,
"It's because of the Jews. Everyone hates the Jews." And he laughed
really hard. He used to really love laughing about how much people
hated Jews.

CHAPTER 39

Author: When Louis said every Arab country, I guess that was an exaggeration?

Noam: Yes, I didn't. I'll tell you the story. I took a semester abroad in Israel in 1983 and we went to Egypt and everybody treated us with amazing hospitality, and then Hassan, who you've interviewed, he found out I was in Egypt. Somehow he found out and he called his family, and his brother called every hotel in Cairo until he found us, and he showed up at the hotel and took us ... We'd never met him ... He took us on this grand tour around Cairo, and on a boat on the Nile, then back to their humble apartment and we had like a seven-course dinner. This was Arab hospitality ... I wouldn't even say on steroids because I believe that may be typical Arab hospitality. It was amazing generosity and they knew I was Jewish. So that was, I'm sure, the story that I told Louis.

CHAPTER 38

Hassan: I said, "Manny, listen to me, you're my boss." He said, "Yes." I said to him, "If you give me the order, any order, and I say no to you, what are you going to do to me?" He said, "You can't say no to me because I'm the boss." I said, "I'm asking you what you're going to do to me. I know you're my boss." He said, "Maybe I will fire you." I said to Manny, "Imagine if you don't believe in God from the beginning? What's God going to give to you? I'll tell you what he's going to give to you. First, he's going to put you in the hell. But where in the hell? Did you see this grill?" You know the grill when we cook the shish kebab?

Author: No. Just say it again. God's going to put you in hell, but where in hell? Is it a place close to the sun or something?

Hassan: Yeah. He's going to put you in the hell. Which place? You know the grill when we cook the shish kebab?

Author: Yeah.

Hassan: When you cook the picnic, you have something to cook the shish kebab, the barbecue, like you have the fire on top and you have the bits of wood come from the material, and then come the stone on top of this.

Author: Where it's white and hottest?

Hassan: Yes. You will be under all this. You're not going to come past. No way.

Author: So why do you get put there? Just for not believing God? For being an apostate?

Hassan: Yes.

Author: Was it a particularly bad place because he was Jewish?

Hassan: No, not because he's Jewish. Because he doesn't believe Allah.

Author: Okay. And how did Manny react to that?

Hassan: He's laughing.

CHAPTER 37

Noam: This guy Bill Grundfest came in and said, you know, "I'll bring comedians, you take the bar, I'll take the door."

Author: Okay. Who's Bill Grundfest?

Noam: He was a comedian. He went on to become the head writer on *Mad About You*. He was a young guy at the time who was, you know, he had a good idea. You can contact him. I can get you his email if you want?

CHAPTER 36

Author: With Marc Maron then, you wouldn't book him, would you? And did he complain about that in person?

Bill Grundfest: Sure. Sure. Oh, he cursed me out something fierce.

Author: Where did that happen?

Bill: The Comedy Cellar. Well, at some point he was like … Why would you go to a place … Even Marc Maron wouldn't go to a place specifically just to curse somebody out, I mean, that would be odd behavior, but no, listen, what he was doing, it didn't work in the room. This room was a positive energy place. One of the common denominators of all of the acts, and it's continued, it is still part of the DNA of the club, everybody has got a positive energy. Nobody is working that angry. There's only one comic that has any hint of anger, you know, like real anger, and that's Allan Havey. And I'm not sure why he has always worked well in the room. I think people feel his essential niceness and so, the anger, they're not really threatened by it. But Marc Maron's anger? That's unfiltered. That's unbridled. That's just pure rage. That's, "Here, let me spew." And I would say, "It's not therapy Marc."

Author: Did you say that to him?

Bill: Yes. "It's not a therapy session where you get to share your rage.

It's not like inverted ..." Some comedians think that this is inverted group therapy. In group therapy you have a group of patients and one therapist. In stand-up comedy you have a group of therapists and one patient. It's not that.

CHAPTER 35

Bill: The number of people who like me versus the number of people who don't are going to be highly correlated with the number of people that I booked on a regular basis, and who felt that I supported them in their careers, and the number of people who don't feel that way. I remember one time … One time three women comedians attacked Manny, not physically, but it was in the Olive Tree, and they got their gumption together and they confronted him about not … It was really weird, because they didn't confront me about it, they confronted him about it, and he wasn't really involved. And they confronted him about not booking them, "You don't book us because we're women." And Manny said, "No," very calmly, "we don't book you because you're not funny."

Author: Oomph.

Bill: And what you just did, oomph, is what I just did. And it's what I did when I was standing there, I went oomph. And they were flabbergasted. They were flabbergasted that someone had said that to them.

CHAPTER 34

Author: You just mentioned Henriette Mantel there as well. I was in touch with Henriette. She had this funny story which Bill told me originally, which is when they confronted Manny and said that he wasn't giving them stage time because they were women. And Henriette had this good line which was … They had a big argument and Henriette said she wouldn't speak to him again unless it was at Camp David. I wondered if you could remember that or anything like that?

Judy Gold: I don't know if I blocked it out, but it was a bad time for women comics, because most clubs wouldn't put two women on the same show. So, if there was one woman on the show, that was the quota.

CHAPTER 33

Bill's on stage,

Bill: This is a great world to be a comedian in, because you don't have to write any jokes. All you have to do is just tell people what's really going on. It's unbelievable the shit that really goes on. You couldn't make it up. Especially here in New York. Just pick up a newspaper. If you can't find a newspaper, just pick up the *Post*. It's an interesting city. Really. Am I right? The shit that goes on in this town. You couldn't make this shit up. If you took acid you could not make up the things that go on in New York. We had ... I'll give you examples. We had people here from Muncie, Indiana, a family that got caught in a gunfight in front of St Patrick's Cathedral. You know these people? The headline in the *Post* the next day, "We still love New York." This is how smart people from Indiana are. "We still love ..." If a New Yorker went to Indiana? Forget a gunfight. Steps in a cow pie? The headline next day would be, "Fuck this place." Really, it's unbelievable what's going on in this world. And just to prove it, allow me to read from *The Satanic Verses* now shall we? This is unbelievable. George Bush said that the Ayatollah's death sentence was offensive. He said it was offensive. The guy hires a hitman for $5.2 million. It's offensive. "Mr. Rushdie, you have just been assassinated, how do you feel?" "I am deeply offended."

CHAPTER 32

Author: That sounds pretty good, University of Pennsylvania, then New York State bar. So why didn't you become a lawyer? Did you do it for a few months?

Noam: I did a few months in LA at a firm which disbanded called Buchalter, Nemer, Fields and Younger. It was a pretty good firm in LA but I can remember specifically when I decided I didn't want to be a lawyer. The way it works is, after your second year in law school you get a job with a law firm. It's called summer clerking, and typically you work there for a few months, and if they like you then they make you an offer of employment after your third year of law school. So it's a very important thing, who you clerk with as a summer clerk, and it's a pretty intense interviewing process. So I got this job with this firm.

Author: In?

Noam: In LA. They did entertainment work.

Author: So you wanted to get into entertainment pretty early?

Noam: I thought it would be fun. So they're trying to induce you to want to take a job with this firm, and this firm's big selling point, and the reason they thought this was the place you ought to work as opposed to the guy down the block, was that after seven years of being partner you were given a one-year sabbatical with pay to do whatever you want. I'm not sure if you understand what that means. Usually you're associate for seven years and then after you're an associate, if you make partner after seven years, you're a partner for seven years. So basically after fourteen, fifteen years, then this big pot of gold is you can have a year to do what you want. I had grown up in a house where my father always did what he wanted. Always. Always. Always. And that's kind of what I said. I said, "This is not for me. At least I ought to exhaust other possibilities before I get on this treadmill here, because I'm not used to that, you know, I don't want to punch a clock like that." So that's when I decided I didn't want to be a lawyer.

CHAPTER 31

Hassan: Manny called me at eight o'clock in the morning. He knows I work all night until seven o'clock. So he called me and he said, "Are you asleep?" So I got like really scared. I said, "What happened?" Because I know he always called me if he has a problem at the Olive Tree. So he said, "Nothing happened. Did you hear the news?" I said, "Manny, I'm sleeping, what's wrong?" He said, "Leave the bed and come back to me now. I'm going to meet you in the Olive Tree." I said, "Manny, I'm asleep. I've only had two hours' sleep." He said, "I'm asking you, come to me." So I went to the Olive Tree thinking, "God, what's the problem? Is it a big problem? Bad problem? So we're going to have a fight?" Because I always fight with him, but fight for the work. Always I fight with Manny in the work. Like, fight personally? We hate each other personally? No, no, no. You understand?

Author: Yes.

Hassan: So anyway, I went to the Olive Tree and he gives me like a big punch in my chest. He says, "Congratulations." I say, "For what?" He says, "Reagan says illegal people here before '82, he can have the green card."

CHAPTER 30

Author: I really loved this thing Hassan told me, which was that immigration officers came to the Olive Tree and arrested him or took him away with Little Ali, and you were a big part of this story. The way Hassan describes it is about four immigration officers came in, they took him away because he didn't have his papers. You were waving over to him, trying to get his attention, trying to get him to leave the Olive Tree, but he didn't and they got him. And then they took him to the immigration building and Manny got him a lawyer. You told him not to say anything until the lawyer arrived, and while he was in there, you were in a McDonald's across the road and you waited for him. Later in the day, after the lawyer arrived to help, Hassan came out of the building, you went up to him and hugged him and he said you said, and I'm sure this was you being nice, "Hassan, don't worry, even if I have to go to Egypt and marry you myself we'll do it, we'll make sure you're not going to get deported."

Ava: I don't remember that. He would remember. We were just trying to make him feel better, yeah, like you said.

Author: Does that sound about right? Do you remember the immigration people coming to the Olive Tree?

Ava: Yes, I remember the immigration people coming. I don't remember that whole second part that you told me, but it sounds right. It sounds like ... Manny loved him so much.

CHAPTER 29

Author: Hassan also told me this other amazing story which happened around that same time, which was that he paid $5,000 to a woman …

Ava: I can't believe he told you that. Oh my god. He did, yes.

Author: He paid $5,000 to this woman who hooked him up with another woman who he went and married, but he took his marriage certificate and birth certificate along with the woman to the immigration office. He described it as a judge, I'm not sure it really was a judge, but this person started going through their documents and came to, I think, her birth certificate, and looked at this certificate and said it didn't look right. So he said, "Come back in a couple of hours, I just need to check it." So you and Hassan and the woman he'd married went and sat in the McDonald's again and the woman said, "I'll be back in five minutes." She went to go to the bathroom, but disappeared. But the immigration office had all Hassan's documents and he didn't know what to do. It was obvious he'd married this woman for what he described as "business," but in the end he went back to the immigration office and made some sort of deal which I couldn't quite understand, but they said, "If the people who sorted you out with this marriage get in touch again let us know, otherwise you're free to go." And they didn't deport him.

Ava: That's exactly right.

CHAPTER 28

Author: Did you lose your $5,000?

Hassan: No, no my friend. I did something ... You're going to laugh, but I'm very mad. Five thousand is big money from my balance. I used to open the Olive Tree, so before I opened, and nobody in the street, like seven o'clock in the morning, I sit in the chair in front of the big window in the Olive Tree, and I saw the woman.

Author: The woman who introduced you to the woman you married? The one you paid the $5,000 to?

Hassan: Yeah, so I said, "Come, I want to talk to you." She came in and we sat by the window and I closed the door. After she sat I brought the shawarma knife. It's true.

Author: Right.

Hassan: And then I went to her, I said, "Listen, I want to tell you something. You know you make me so I'm married to a girl? Is she married before? I don't know what happened, but anyway, she married with a fake certificate." I first got very red, understand? So I said, "I don't care about this. Only what I care about is my money. Because now if you don't give me my money, you going to be the end of your life. I do something very bad for you and I leave because I'm leaving anyway. So give me my money." She said, "Hassan, it's no

321

problem, I will give you the money, but let me use the phone." She said, "I'm going to ask in front of you, a girl who lives with me to bring the money." She called the girl, she bring the money. I take my money. I said, "Okay, I take the money. Now I know you live in front of me, but do me big favor, I don't want to see you here anymore. You don't lose anything. I don't lose anything. Bye, bye, bye, bye." And I take my money back.

CHAPTER 27

Author: You said that someone heckled you on the stage at the Cellar, do you remember what that man said?

Carol Siskind: I'm trying to … I know my response was … I said, "It's hard for you seeing a powerful woman up here, isn't it?" I remember that was my response, because very much in that moment I got it and I don't … I'm trying to remember. I don't think it was about my appearance, but it may have been, because you know, that was a big thing for women back then, how you dressed, what you look like. I mean it still is for a woman, let's face it. That's the first thing people see and … You know, I had a friend who was very well-endowed and she would dress in these huge sweatshirts, you know, she was trying to draw attention away from her bust, so that was always an issue. I'm trying to remember what he said. I think it was more a comment on some of my material.

Author: So his comment hasn't stuck with you, but what you said to him has, and you think it was, "It's hard for you to see a powerful woman up here"?

Carol: Yes. As a woman, making an audience laugh puts you in a very powerful position.

CHAPTER 26

Author: You said you got into stand-up because there weren't very many female comedians, so you thought it was an opportunity for you, and I really want to focus on the Cellar ...

Rita Rudner: I wish I could remember more, I just remember the chairs weren't very comfortable and I drank a lot of Diet Coke.

Author: Do you remember Manny Dworman?

Rita: Who? I'm sorry?

Author: Manny Dworman, the man who owned it.

Rita: Oh, I remember him slightly, but Bill Grundfest was the one person who was there all the time. He was the one who ran it. He was the one responsible for scheduling and everything.

Author: And with Bill did it feel like a place where women were welcome and you were given equal opportunity there?

Rita: Absolutely, yeah, because a new comedy club has to welcome comedians who were doing well in the area and he was a nice guy. And he was very affable, so everybody liked to ... He was happy all the time.

Author: Bill told me a story about three female comedians who complained they weren't getting booked because they were women, and he used you as an example. He said he booked Rita Rudner every opportunity he could possibly get. I think he said he stalked you to get you to do more spots there.

Rita: He did, yeah, and he was nice to me. Absolutely. But I think you have to earn your keep there. And I already had a reputation around town, and I was making people laugh, and I was getting on local TV shows and the David Letterman show. I was somebody who he could count on to be funny when I got on stage.

CHAPTER 25

Vic Henley: Quinn was just the funniest guy in the world. And I always remember that if you bombed or it didn't go well, Quinn was always there to say the right thing. He was always there to … "These people are fucking stupid. Don't pay any attention. That was not you. That's them. They're fucking stupid. That goddam … That Copernicus reference." That's Colin. The hardest thing in comedy Andrew, the only thing that you cannot teach in comedy, is to not give a fuck. They can't teach that. You just have to innately not give a fuck. Otherwise you will be a nervous wreck based on every laugh or not laugh that the audience gives or takes away from you.

CHAPTER 24

Jon Manfrellotti: Grenada was some, like, tropical island where America had a university or something, and some people, some terrorists or something were holding the students hostage. So we sent in some troops and the whole campaign lasted about ten minutes, you know. They freed everybody. And I was on stage one night and it was in the news and I probably wouldn't have done this joke if I hadn't been watching the news earlier in the day, and I said, "You know we attacked Grenada? That's like attacking Club Med, you know what I mean. People are on the beach putting suntan lotion on, 'Honey, is that a submarine?'" And that's all I said, you know, and some guy stood up and said, "My buddy was there and he got wounded." But that was it. That was it. You know what I mean?

CHAPTER 23

Author: I wondered whether you could think of a time when you said a joke at the Comedy Cellar which annoyed people or outraged people at all? Do you think there's anything you said on the stage which had a bad reaction?

Gilbert Gottfried: Well, it's like, back in those days, the very worst ... I mean, when people would go ... Sometimes people would hiss.

CHAPTER 22

Ava: We would have to take flak at the door sometimes from customers that weren't happy with what the comedians said. I remember that, because Manny and I and Estee and people would always be at the door and somebody would be like, "Oh, my god, what's going to happen now?" Maybe somebody would say something and we'd say nicely, you know, "We understand, but that's the art of comedy."

Author: Somebody said an interesting thing, which was that if a customer was angry sometimes Manny would talk to them, but sometimes he'd send you instead if it was a man, because it would defuse them better. It would deescalate things.

Ava: I don't even think it was because it was a man. I feel if it was anyone, because we both had that big empathetic gene in us. And I really did understand. They knew that I meant it from my heart that I was sorry they felt that way. That's it. Not only that, but in the beginning there was no security people at the door. Sometimes I'd run to Manny for back-up but it was much easier to talk to people. It was more about talking to people. Just listening and talking.

CHAPTER 21

Author: Regarding your dad's views on like, political correctness, freedom of speech and things like that, have you got any kinds of recordings of him or any kind of documentary evidence of him ever writing about it?

Noam: No, I don't, but this is what you have to remember, in those days, that was the liberal opinion too. The American Civil Liberties Union, the gold standard of liberal views, went to court to defend the Nazis, their right to march on Skokie. They would never do that today. I actually … On one of my podcasts they had the former head of the Civil Liberties Union on, I don't know if you heard it, and he said he didn't think they would do it today. So when my father had those views about people being able to say whatever they want, and should say whatever they want, and let's have a debate, let's get a Holocaust denier in here, this was mainstream, and if anything, liberal views. I mean, you have to live through it to shudder at how it's changed. When I went to college they invited Meir Kahane and Noam Chomsky and I mean any kind of radical guy. Nobody cared. Nobody cared. And they spoke and we saw the lectures and they were interesting and we didn't become Nazis. But now, I know how he would feel about this, but it wasn't an issue then, there was nobody saying anything about trigger warnings or anything like that.

CHAPTER 20

Author: I interviewed Mark Cohen.

Rick Crom: How'd you get him to concentrate for more than ten minutes?

Author: He was great actually, he was really good.

Rick: He's wonderful. Very talented.

Author: And he mentioned, when he first came here he was doing ...

Rick: He did a guitar act.

Author: And he said one of the songs upset you a little bit, because it was kind of ...

Rick: Homophobic? Yeah, there was something that he did.

Author: "Queen of the Road" I think it was? He camped it up a little bit.

Rick: Yeah, yeah, yeah. Well, you have to remember, at that time I was ... I was only hypersensitive because I didn't want to be a gay comedian. I just wanted to be a comedian. And there were a lot of us who were out in our regular lives but not on stage. So people who were overtly … It was just, like, it was cheap. It's stupid. It upset me more then than it would upset me now. Now I just go, "Really? The campy voice?" Manny would go, "It's funny." "Yes, it is funny, so is doing a Jewish actor going, 'Such a deal, such a deal, such a deal.' That's funny too, isn't it? Or doing a minstrel show? That's funny too, yeah?" But back then … Back then doing … Doing gay jokes was perfectly fine, you know. You're talking … You could do … On TV you could do Polish jokes. They would use the word, "Two Polacks this …" Johnny Carson would do it. Then the Polish League Against Defamation went, "Stop that." So anyway, I was a little hypersensitive back then in a way I wouldn't be now.

Author: And Mark thought he stopped getting booked for a little bit because of it. Like, only a month or something like that. Then he talked to Estee and explained, and I think he stopped doing it actually.

Rick: Well, I mean, I didn't like Mark Cohen at all when he first came in. I didn't like him and I think it's because, in retrospect, he was doing a music act.

CHAPTER 19

Mark Cohen: They loved me and I worked for like a week or so there. She put me instantly on the wall there and then they stopped using me. And I went up to them and I said, "Why did you stop using me?" And it was because Rick Crom complained about me. Rick's a really good friend of mine by the way, and we ended up becoming very close and performing together. But I used to do this ... It's really not offensive. I used to do a parody of "King of the Road" called "Queen of the Road." I mean, it's nothing I'm necessarily proud of, but it wasn't angry against homosexuals. But he took offense at it.

CHAPTER 18

Charles Zucker: I was just playing the piano. It was a baby grand and the piano had a … I don't know if Bill told you this. It had a Plexiglass cover on it and Bill would as a joke sometimes pick it up and use it as a shield. He'd say, "Oh, I need a shield" when the audience was being hostile or mean to him or something. So one night there was a couple who wouldn't shut up. They were just nasty, they wouldn't shut up and Bill was really patient, trying to get them to quiet down, and it's not my proudest moment but I had the microphone at the piano and in sort of a low but loud voice I said, "Can somebody please put a dick in her mouth?"

Author: Bill's told me the story but it'd be great for the book to hear it from you.

Charles: So they went nuts. Bill puts up the audience shield as a joke and the next thing you know, silverware and ashtrays and dishes are flying at the stage and it looked like mayhem. And Bill was very gracious, and the woman and the guy were like, asked to leave, and she starts screeching something like, "I've never been treated this badly in my whole life," and Bill says, "When you behave with some civility you'll be treated in kind." And the audience applauds and they leave and they go out in the hall. And I'm sure Bill told you, the next thing I know, it was a little hazy, but out of the corner of my eye I see that Bill's feet are no longer touching the ground because this guy has his hands around his neck and he's choking him.

CHAPTER 17

Bill: I needed the best comics that I could get, so the question is, how can you attract them? How can you get them to come from uptown? And one way is to pay them a little more, so that they have cab fares, as well as they're able to put ten bucks in their pocket, but that is in addition to what I was describing yesterday, with creating a home. These guys are by definition lone wolves. They do what they do in isolation. They're stand-up comedians. They write their own material. They perform by themselves and they're solitary, but by creating a place that was warm and welcoming … We gave them a club house, and said to them, "Come and experiment …" See, that's another thing, the uptown clubs, Catch, Comic Strip, the Improv, you had to kill every set, and with us, we would say, "If you want to kill every set, that's what the uptown clubs are for. Here, this is your gym. Experiment. If we believe in you, we think that even your bombing will be interesting."

CHAPTER 16

Bill: What I said to Manny was, if anybody who's coming for the Brazilian piano bar comes early, before ten o'clock, I'm not going to charge them a cover charge, they're welcome to come in. And if any of our audience wants to stay, then they'll stay. But it wasn't but a few months before the piano player had to find another bar to work in.

CHAPTER 15

Bill: I was really nervous because I needed to find some place, and I walked past a couple of times because I just kept looking at this dank staircase and, "Oh, it's just so icky." But then I said to myself, "Places that aren't icky, you're not going to be able to get." So then I went in the Olive Tree and I asked to see the owner and as luck would have it he was there and I showed him this review.

Author: Was he sitting at a table?

Bill: No, I told the hostess, who ... I forget who it was who I approached. And they came back with him, so he was at the front and, you know, I asked him what he was doing with the room downstairs and he told me a Brazilian piano bar. And I said, "Well, what time do you do?" Because, you know, perhaps somebody else would have said, "Sorry for bothering you." But I was just looking for any opening. So, "What time do you start at?" "Oh, ten o'clock." "Okay, so, you know, I would like to do this comedy club from eight to ten, and we'll have a cover and a minimum and I'll pay the comics and I'll pay to get an audience in and to promote it and you serve food and beverage, and it's extra food and beverage. If a lot of people come, great, and if not a lot of people come, fine. There's no way for you to lose. It's only a question of how much you can win."

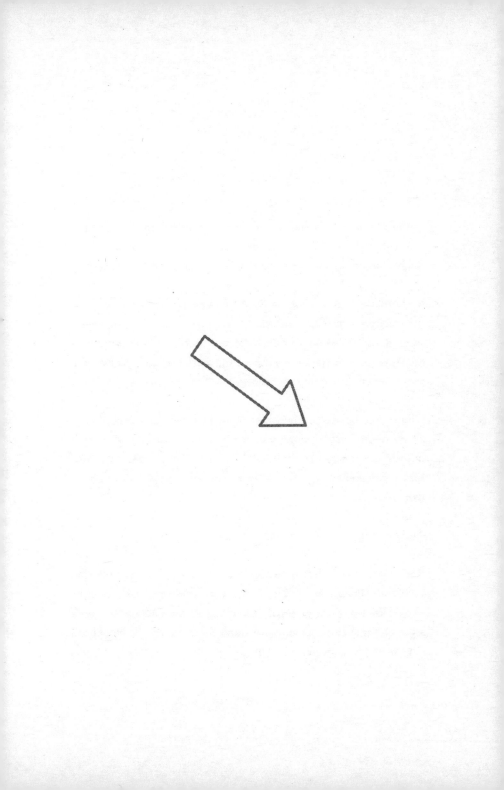

CHAPTER 14

Author: I know your dad's a civil rights lawyer, so I read his book.

Rachel Feinstein: That was crazy that you read my dad's book.

Author: He mentions Don Imus and other people who used language that backfired on them, and your dad doesn't seem very happy with what these people said. I wondered if he'd ever disagreed with any of the language that you or any other comedians use, and whether you ever talked to him about that at all?

Rachel: No, no, he … I mean, he has a dark, weird sense of humor. That's where I get a lot of my sense of humor. Like, he would come in the room and be like, "It smells like Jews in here. It's really gross." Like, "Can you guys get out of the room?" He would say things like that.

Author: When you were a kid?

Rachel: Yeah, yeah, he would jokingly sing, "Last train to Auschwitz, I shall see you at the …" Things like that. And my mom would be like, "Howard, that's enough." So he had always had a weird, dark sense of humor, and sometimes I think that's the way he would call out the preposterousness of all of it.

CHAPTER 13

Author: You've said there were lots of anti-Haitian jokes when you were growing up. Why were they telling anti-Haitian jokes?

Wil Sylvince: I guess they didn't like Haitians or thought they just, you know … I don't know the reason why people pick on each other when they don't understand a culture or religion or a thing or can't relate. They just make fun of it. Plus, you know, another thing has to do with Haitians, we didn't have like a hero to make us look cool. For example the Chinese had Bruce Lee, the Jamaicans had Bob Marley. So we didn't have like a cool figure, so it was easy to make jokes of us, you know what I'm saying, because no one wanted to be Haitian. The things that we had about us were negative stereotypes and some of them aren't true. For example, there's some cool stereotypes, like Asians know how to do math and they know kung-fu. Black people have big penises. But then we had that we do voodoo, we wore mismatched clothes, or the worst one was probably Haitians had AIDS.

Author: Do you remember any of the jokes?

Wil: One of the jokes … I remember a few of them. "What do you call Haitians on skates? Rolaids." "What do you call a Haitian band? Band-Aids." Jokes like that.

Author: And did children tell those jokes to you knowing you were Haitian?

Wil: Yeah.

Author: And something I've read is, your dad told you just to pretend to be Jamaican because that would make your life easier. Is that true?

Wil: No, you got that wrong. My dad did not say that. Actually, my parents were very proud to be Haitian. I came up with that when I went to a different school district and I had … It was almost like a new take on life, a new start on life, and I figured I could have a new identity by just pretending to be something I wasn't.

CHAPTER 12

Keith: Ain't nothing changed.

Author: Did people say stuff about your sneakers?

Keith: Absolutely, but they know I would get them. Eventually I would get them. One thing … I thought about this. That I didn't realize I was bullying. Like a lot of guys … One guy … Used to talk about him so bad and he punched me right in my face.

Author: He punched you?

Keith: Yeah.

Author: What did you say to him?

Keith: I kept calling him schizo-fag. Like, one minute you're gay, one minute you're straight. It was a good chuckle. Everybody laughed. I was like, "Ah, this is good."

Author: Where was that? At the back of the bus?

Keith: In school, in the back of the classroom, also was … The teacher said, "Keith, go to the back of the room, you're not going to learn, you just want to make fun, get your ass to the back." And I'm smiling and I was, "Hey, hey, schizo-fag." Guys are laughing. We're just having a good time. But I didn't realize back then that was a form of bullying. A girl, I used to always mess with her. Like I would do the Beverly Hillbillies song, "Black gold, Texas tea," because she was real dark. That, "Hey there lonely girl," I'd say, "Hey there ugly girl." I would just fuck with her so bad, right? I would fuck with her so bad and like … I mean really bad. I was fucking with her, seventh grade, eighth grade, ninth grade.

Author: Did she cry?

Keith: Oh, you didn't see how bad it was. I was out of school now, graduated high school and all that. I was maybe nineteen at a church, sat there, Bethel Baptist Church, and I'm sitting there and she starts kicking my chair. Boom. I'm like, "What the hell? Who's kicked my chair?" It was her, making faces at me, just angry. She was still hurt from sixth, seventh grade.

Author: When was that?

Keith: I was nineteen then. I was only thirteen, fourteen when I was teasing her. And she was in there kicking my chair. I'm like, "Huh? Hey." "Fuck you." "What? We're in church." She hated my guts.

Author: Did you apologize to her?

Keith: No, because you don't know. And I'm like, "Why is she so mad? I was just joking with her." But you don't know the effect you can have on people.

CHAPTER 11

Hood: Let's call us persecuted, is probably the right word. If you do a "Bahai Iran persecution" Google search you will see some horrific things that started about one hundred years ago and continue to today. So as a religious minority, persecuted religious minority, it just made sense for my family at the time to kind of send us off to boarding school, and to relocate after boarding school to the US. We initially came over here because my father was doing some ... He has a doctorate in veterinary medicine. He was doing some research at the university in Maryland on bees and honey bees specifically. So that's what landed us here. And in 1979 Iran started to, you know ... It had fifty or so more guests than maybe it should for a little while and that whole hostage thing led to an increase in the persecution, because of the Ayatollah takeover, and we were able to very justifiably claim religious persecution and head down the track of US citizenship.

CHAPTER 10

Hassan: When I left from Cairo, my mother, she said to me, "Hassan, I know there are a lot of Jewish people in America, so watch. Be careful."

CHAPTER 9

Noam: He always let me read and see whatever I wanted. There was absolutely no … He used to get a lot of flak from other parents and stuff like that. I remember I was reading *The Exorcist* at eleven years old, the woman at the drug store started screaming at him. And also, even more memorable, he took me to see *Straw Dogs*. Have you ever seen *Straw Dogs* with Dustin Hoffman? You know that rape scene? When did it come out, 1969 or something? It was rated R, so he was allowed to take me, and the woman at the box office didn't want to let me in and he was screaming at her, "It's none of your fucking business."

CHAPTER 8

Author: What was it that your dad liked about debating?

Noam: Say again?

Author: Just if you could explain why did he want to debate with people? What was it that he valued about debate? Was it a sport thing to him? Or was he trying to get to the truth? What was it?

Noam: Yeah, it's just interesting to him. You know, when it came to Israel it was the most important thing to him. But on other matters, it's just a very, you know, he was like a public intellectual type.

Author: And how did that kind of evolve at the Cellar, at the Olive Tree? Did he do it a little bit at the start? Did he ever talk about it?

Noam: He's always been like that. He's just been like that since I was born. It's just who he always was.

Author: Did he ever talk to you about it? About how much he enjoyed it?

Noam: No.

Author: So it's just something that he did and it wasn't something he talked about?

Noam: Andrew, you sound like such a Gentile. I'm trying to realize how to explain this stuff to you, because it's just so, like, not unusual in a Jewish atmosphere. It's like I'm trying to understand why … I know it's my fault. I'm making assumptions that … I really have to understand I'm making assumptions. This is just the way Jewish people are. You heard me quoting that verse from *Fiddler on the Roof*?

Author: Yeah. Well, what is it?

Noam: In the song, "If I Were a Rich Man," he has a whole song about it, "If I were rich I'd have this and I'd have one staircase going up and one staircase …" All these material things. But that's not really the point of the song, and in the last verse he says, you can look it up, "If I were rich I'd have the time that I lack to sit in the synagogue and pray, and maybe have a seat by the Eastern Wall, and I'd discuss the holy books with the learned men several hours every day, that would be the sweetest thing of all." Meaning that the true pleasure of being rich would be to sit around and discuss the holy books, to debate, because that's … Like, a Talmudic debate is, "What about this? What about that? This rabbi thinks it's this way. This rabbi interprets it this way." So this is like the highest … This would be the goal of being wealthy and just traditional Jewish culture would be to have that leisure time to do precisely what it is that we're talking about, to discuss the current day version of holy books with the learned men. So when you're discussing the law and civil liberties with Alan Dershowitz, it's a very American version of discussing the holy books with the learned men, that's what it is.

CHAPTER 7

Noam: You don't know what a Fuller Brush man is do you? A door-to-door brush salesman. He was a cab driver, he was a merchant seaman, he taught English at a foreign language school at Berlitz. He did a lot of these types of jobs and I guess the last one, he was a cab driver. He opened a little tiny coffee shop on Seventh Avenue called the Feenjon.

Author: So he earned enough driving a cab to put capital down?

Noam: Yeah, you know, I think he got some financial help from his father maybe, but his father was a pauper, so it was … In those days you could open a business from scratch with almost nothing, and he had nothing, a few hundred dollars here and a few hundred dollars there. You can't do that anymore and that's terrible, but in any case, that's how he started, and it wasn't a nightclub, it was a coffee shop.

Author: How do you spell it?

Noam: F-E-E-N-J-O-N.

Author: What does it mean?

Noam: It's the Turkish coffee pots with a long handle, that's called a Feenjon, but it's also somehow symbolic of, you know, peace and friendship.

Author: It was on Seventh Avenue?

Noam: Yeah, Seventh Avenue and Commerce Street I think.

Author: In Greenwich Village?

Noam: Yeah, it's in the Village, but it's like, the outskirts of the popular parts of the Village. It's a little bit out of the way.

Author: Selling coffee and Danishes?

Noam: Coffee and who knows. I wasn't even born, but what made this place special was he and his friends used to play music there informally at the tables, and very quickly all kinds of musicians were coming down there all the time.

Author: In the 1950s?

Noam: This is 1960.

Author: 1960 he opened it?

Noam: Yeah, my father had a lot of Middle Eastern and Israeli musicians, they would all come down, but also Dylan would come down and José Feliciano performed there, and it became very, very popular, very, very quickly.

Author: Bob Dylan?

Noam: Yeah, Bob Dylan. My father knew Dylan.

Author: Really? Okay. That's quite a big deal isn't it?

Noam: I guess. You know, it's hard for me to have perspective about it, because it's always been that way. I remember much later in, like, the mid-Seventies, Dylan came into the Olive Tree and he said, "Manny, you're still king." Like that. It made him feel good.

CHAPTER 6

Manny Dworman,

Informality was the rule. Very often I would sit down among the coffee drinkers and chess players with my guitar and mandolin to accompany one or another of the many musicians who wandered in. Gradually, more and more musicians came to look upon the Feenjon as their second home.

CHAPTER 5

Author: So your dad was kind of, I'm not sure if this is the right word, but a beatnik?

Noam: No, not at all. Exactly the opposite actually. He's contradictions, because he smoked pot every day of his life. He always smoked pot. On the other hand he was a totally conservative guy. He always hated the Sixties. He always hated the hippie culture. He really did. He always, always felt it was a phoney thing.

CHAPTER 4

Manny,

Though I was born in Israel, I was raised in Brooklyn, New York. Israeli music was always a part of my life as was Russian music, since both my parents were born in Russia. My musical career began at the age of twelve with the ocarina, or "sweet potato," (an instrument I like to think of as native to Brooklyn) and later went to the mandolin, the guitar, and then, the oud. During my college days, I shared a room with a Greek-American by the name of Bill Bouris. He introduced me to Greek music but also opened up for me the whole world of Middle Eastern music.

CHAPTER 3

Author: You said that stuff about Louis CK, that it's so small, like, there are hundreds of millions of people around the world so interested in this thing, they think it's such a big deal, but actually it's really, really small. And you said that thing about, you know, you've got a microscope and you just keep zooming in and zooming in until the problems become bigger and bigger. So I'm trying to reflect ... This is something that Estee talked about, her grandparents she said were shot in the Holocaust. I know your dad was in Israel during the Holocaust but I didn't know ...

Noam: No, he was in America during the Holocaust.

Author: In America sorry. I didn't know if he had any relatives who were killed in the Holocaust?

Noam: Not to my knowledge. Not to my knowledge.

Author: So the Holocaust didn't affect you guys in a direct way?

Noam: Well I think you're putting too much emphasis on what it meant to be a Jew in the Forties regardless of whether somebody you knew had died or not. They killed six million Jews. I think everybody was directly affected by it. I doubt there's much difference in the way people were affected by the ... I mean, if someone lost their mother, that's a thing, but this was ... I wouldn't put too much stock in that distinction.

Author: Sure, okay. So did he ever talk to you about that? Did he ever talk about how he felt about it?

Noam: About the Holocaust?

Author: Yes.

Noam: He was against it.

CHAPTER 2

Author: You talked about how some of your family was killed in the Holocaust.

Estee: Most of my family. Most of my family. My mother and her two brothers survived. Everybody else ... My mother had another brother, her parents, and extended family. I never met my grandparents. So most of them were lost in the Holocaust. The Holocaust is an extremely sensitive point with me. A lot of people move on. And I don't. I don't think I am allowed to. Somebody has to remember. You know what I mean? And I am the next generation and so I am a very close witness to what the Holocaust did to people, and just the way my mother was ... My step-father ... My step-father was a married man with a son, with brothers, sisters. That guy was left alone. Not a cousin on the planet. Everybody was exterminated. So it does something to your personality. It makes you sensitive and it makes you angry and it makes you ... That was watching them, you know ... What is the word I'm trying to ... like, inferiority complex. All of those emotions together create a certain type of individual, and so that's where I came from.

Author: Was your father killed in the Holocaust?

Estee: No. My mother was hiding with him during the Holocaust with the partisans in the forest and the farmlands. They were moving for three years in Poland. The winters are so extreme, I can't tell you, and they were just on the move. They were in a concentration camp for a very short time. They escaped.

Author: Your mother was?

Estee: Yeah, they escaped. It wasn't one of the major ones. So they did all of that. The partisans and the hiding with the farmers, paying off farmers, and there was a hole and they were inside that hole. I mean, I cannot imagine how you survive that. I can't, because my mother, if she had a hangnail, it was like, "Ow, ow, ow." I said, "Ma, you went through the Holocaust, I don't get it," but yeah, it's a time that I was blessed that I was born after, but the after-effect of it I felt because I lived with my mother and the night terrors, when she would wake up in the middle of the night and stuff like that, you know. Her brother, who is her junior, he was thirteen I think during the war, and it's funny how both of them, they remember the same events differently. He says she's wrong and she says, "Well, he was a child, what does he know?" Their parents got executed right away.

Author: Do you know where?

Estee: Poland.

Author: In a camp? Or shot in the street?

Estee: I'm Jewish and my grandparents were orthodox, so it was visible who they were. They were known also. And they were executed in the town square.

CHAPTER 1

Estee: I'm not offended by much. I don't mind dirty jokes. What I do mind is hurtful, and without benefit. There's nobody benefits from a Holocaust joke, unless it's somebody that has no idea what the Holocaust is all about. If you're a younger man and don't have a relationship to the Holocaust, you didn't lose anybody, you know it from a book, so you are emotionally disconnected. And for you that's okay. For me it's not because I am emotionally connected.

Author: Do you ever say anything to any of the comedians?

Estee: No.

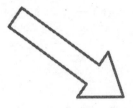

EPILOGUE

Author: You said on the phone the other day you were worried about something I'd asked you about, which was cancel culture, where I said, or implied in one of my questions, that you might be more forgiving of what someone said because you were worried it might happen to you.

Noam: Yeah, I remember that. No, it's not because of that. I've always been that way.

Author: You've always been that way?

Noam: I remember very clearly, when Mel Gibson was in trouble for making that movie ...

Author: Which movie?

Noam: *Passion of the Christ*, which had some blatant anti-Semitic images. As a matter of fact I even wrote a letter that was published in the *Weekly Standard* discussing the blatant anti-Semitism. Also, he had some things on tape, or he said some things about Jews, I don't even remember all the things. It was pretty clear. And I remember thinking that they should let him keep making movies and you can see them or not. I've always been reluctant to embrace the idea of a mob retaliation for something somebody said.

Author: Is that because you think he's going to learn and improve?

Noam: No, I just think it spins out of control and it's arbitrary. It's the … It's quite often unfair. Quite often facts come out a year later that were unknown, and I just don't believe in putting that kind of blood in the water. I think the cure is much worse than the disease, which is not to say that anybody who gets canceled is necessarily not deserving of being canceled. It's to say that when you encourage this kind of retaliation, very, very quickly it's going to become unfair. As I said, the cure will become much worse than the disease, and I think we've seen that already.

Author: A lot of people are fearful of … Particular comedians are fearful now of that kind of culture, where you say the wrong thing so you're branded forever. My agent was over at the Cellar a few weeks ago, he went to see a show, and he said he kind of felt, and he might be wrong, but he felt some of the male comedians were self-censoring. Have you noticed that at all?

Noam: I haven't really. I have to say, I haven't.

Author: So you think people are getting up on the Cellar stage still and saying what they want?

Noam: I mean, I don't want to sound naive, but yeah, I think they are.

Author: Are you still doing that thing with the phones where people have their phones taken off them now? Or is it just for certain shows?

Noam: Yeah we're still doing it.

Author: For all the shows or just some shows?

Noam: All the shows.

Author: You think that's helped, because there's a much smaller chance that anybody in the audience is going to film it and put it online? Do the comedians feel freer to do what they want to do because of that?

Noam: Probably. Probably they do.

Author: Is it not something you've discussed with any of them?

Noam: I haven't heard that from the comedians. I hear that going around. I haven't heard it directly from anybody. But what I have heard from the comedians is they feel the audience is much more in the moment and paying attention. I mean, look at what happened with this guy Shane Gillis and these *Legion of Skanks* comedians. They're not censoring themselves.

Author: Yeah, but it seems like those guys have really had to develop their own audience and, you know, they sacrifice …

Noam: That's what happens. I think that the comedians who are fueled by the kind of in-your-face controversial presentation, they don't know any other way of being, so they just do it and they … Look, and you're right, they develop their own audience, like Andrew Schulz, a comedian I think is terrific, he just takes it directly on YouTube, he has a million followers, he sells out all over the country, and nobody can really touch him.

Author: Okay.

Noam: Look, even Louis … Louis could still sell out Madison Square Garden. Maybe even … The issue would be that people would attack

Madison Square Garden for allowing him to perform there, and that is where we really cross the line into a bad situation, you know, where … And the hypocrisy is obvious. A university can invite virtually any leader in the world. China has a million Muslims in concentration camps. Does anybody object if the leader of China comes to speak somewhere? But Louis CK, who has never even been accused of breaking the law, who's done something he should be ashamed of, is now not permitted to work at venues which leant themselves to the general showbiz industry. It's … I don't see any … It's just a very seat-of-the-pants, make-it-up-as-you-go-along type of procedure.

Author: And at the start, when Louis first came back, you were under pressure, and I remember you had a couple of protestors outside, but you kept allowing him on anyway. Did you have any protestors after that?

Noam: No. Just the two women that one night.

Author: The pressure just dissipated, did it?

Noam: Well, to be accurate, that was the only night that we listed his name on the line-up, a lot of people had criticized me for not listing his name on the line-up so I gave it a shot, suspecting it would blow up in my face, and it didn't work out, so we didn't list him on the line-up anymore. We just did the swim-at-your-own-risk policy. So that was that, and yeah, it dissipated. He hasn't been at the Cellar in a year, but he's touring all over the country and he's selling out everywhere.

Author: Yeah. You had to cancel a debate recently as well? Can you explain that?

Noam: And by the way, Mike Tyson, I've said this a million times,

Bill Clinton and Mike Tyson, who've also been accused or even convicted of things worse than Louis was accused of ... Bill Clinton, he's welcome everywhere. Yeah, we canceled the debate because there was a lot of rumbling on Twitter that people were going to come to disrupt it.

Author: Because of the subject of it?

Noam: Because of the subject matter, yeah.

Author: Which was?

Noam: It was about reparations.

Author: Okay.

Noam: And I just didn't want to put my staff in that kind of risky situation, you know.

Author: You said on the phone a few calls ago, when we talked about the book, that you might not have agreed to do it if I started doing it now, you know, since things have changed. I wondered what's changed? Is it you that's changed? Has the world changed? What's different now?

Noam: Yeah, I just have a whole ... Suddenly ... The book started before Louis, correct?

Author: Yeah, yeah.

Noam: Because this was going to be a nice book about the history of the Comedy Cellar, and now it's a book about, you know, about a confrontation in a sense, and I have a whole PTSD from that whole chapter, you know. I never really recovered from it. It was horrible. So I just don't want anything that could open that wound again.

Author: You say you kind of have PTSD. It affected you badly did it?

Noam: Terrible. I mean, we were getting threats of violence. People who worked for me, who were wearing Comedy Cellar t-shirts, were accosted on the subway.

Author: Really? Did that happen?

Noam: Yeah.

Author: Wow. What do you mean accosted?

Noam: People would say, "How could you work there? Blah, blah, blah." People yelling and screaming. There'd also be … The honesty of the reporters who would take your words and chop them up like a guy snipping out words from a magazine to write a ransom note, and put them together to write whatever story they wanted …

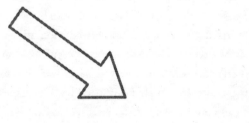

ACKNOWLEDGEMENTS

Author: Right, this book slightly changed for the American edition, so I've adjusted the acknowledgements, but most of this is the same. Firstly, thank you to everyone at the Comedy Cellar, past and present, especially anyone who spoke to me, including Ava Har'el, Elizabeth Furiati, Estee Adoram, Hassan Ragheb, Hatem Gabr, Juanita Dworman, Mohamed El-Taweel and Steve Fabricant. I owe particular thanks to Noam Dworman for all the time he gave me and for letting me hang around his business and visit his home. It took a lot of trust and he didn't stop trusting even when I wrote things he didn't like, nor when he was under pressure for allowing Louis CK back on stage. At that point the book became different to the book I originally intended. I knew he was stressed but he kept making himself available for interviews, which I appreciate. Thanks to some other non-comedians who talked to me, including Anthony Cumia, Christian Charles, David Pettinato, John Cook, Jordan Sargent and Patrick Milligan. Thanks to Erika, Leah and @9amburritos, whose full names I promised to leave out of the book. I know people might be tempted to identify them online, but please don't. Thanks to a few others who helped in some way, including Andy Miller, Christine Evans, Damian Shiels, Dan Shaki, George Rush, Jimmy Thomson, Katie Way, Lee Hurst, MaryAnn Giraldo, Melena Ryzik, Nathan Bransford, Nina Mohanty, Victoria Coren Mitchell and some of the staff at *The Daily Californian* newspaper. Thanks to Elizabeth Widdicombe for commissioning my article about the table for the *New Yorker*. Thanks to Larry Doyle for digging out his notes from over two decades ago. Thanks to Andrew Sullivan for letting me print his words from the debate. Thanks to others who said or published words which appear in this book, including the BBC, Cherrell Brown, Hollywood Reporter, Interrobang, Lena Dunham, Marc Maron, *New York Magazine*, *The New York Times*, *New Yorker* and Sarah Silverman. For the two chapters written by Manny I used copy he wrote for his record sleeves. If you want to read Rachel's dad's book, it's called *Fire on the Bayou* by Howard L. Feinstein. A big thanks to all the comedians I talked to including Aaron Berg, Allan Havey, Andy De La Tour, whose book about New York comedy is called *Stand-Up or Die*. Thanks to Bill Grundfest, Bonnie McFarlane, Carol Siskind, Charles Zucker, Colin Quinn, Dan Naturman, Dan Soder, Dat Phan, DC Benny, Dom Irera, Dov Davidoff, Dustin Chafin, Gary Gulman, Gilbert Gottfried, Godfrey, Greg Fitzsimmons, Gregg Rogell, Guy Branum ... Extra thanks to Guy for letting me use his article. I understood his criticism of the balance of interviewees in my article for the *New Yorker*, and I know there's an imbalance in this book, but it's something I am more aware of now. Thanks to Henriette Mantel, Hood Qaim-Maqami and Jay Oakerson. Regarding Jay, he asked to be completely removed from the book. I didn't do that, but just to provide some clarity, I think Jay is funny. Thanks to Jim Norton, Joe De Rosa, Joe List, Joe Machi, Jon Hayman, Jon Laster, Jon Manfrelloti, Jonathan Solomon, Judd Apatow, Judy Gold, Keith Robinson, Kevin Brennan, Kurt Metzger, Lenny Marcus, Lewis Schaffer, Liza Treyger, Louis CK ... When I was put in touch with Louis CK I promised the person who put me in touch that I would only ask about the Cellar. I know some journalists wouldn't have accepted those terms, but I already had a lot of material about his misconduct from other people, so I thought it was worth speaking to him, and I kept my promise. Thanks to Lynne Koplitz, Mark Cohen, Mark Normand, Mike Royce, Mitch Fatel, Modi, Nick Di Paolo, Paul Mecurio, Rachel Feinstein, Rich Vos, Rick Crom, Rita Rudner, Robert Kelly, Rory Albanese, Russ

Meneve, Ryan Hamilton, Sam Morril, Sherrod Small and Stewart Lee. I did a long interview with Stewart which formed the prologue of the British edition, but what we talked about wouldn't have made sense to a lot of American readers, so we cut it from this edition. I'm hugely appreciative to him, though, and when Americans ask which British comedian they should see I tell them Stewart Lee. Thanks to Ted Alexandro, Tom Papa, Tony Daro, Wali Collins and Wil Sylvince. Sadly, two people I interviewed died before this was published. William Stephenson died in 2019. Vic Henley died in 2020. They were both unique and brilliant. As I said, the book started out as something and ended up as something else, which meant a lot of interview material wasn't used. Similar to jokes, writing this book was a long process of whittling the story down to what I really wanted to say. Even for those who didn't appear in the book, their thoughts impacted what the book ended up being, and I greatly appreciate everybody's time. If you're wondering why I didn't speak to a particular comedian, I probably tried, but lots of people declined, perfectly reasonably, just as some non-comedians didn't respond when I tried to contact them, again perfectly reasonably. If any jokes in this book fall flat or the comedians sound like they're trying to be nasty on stage, that's my fault. To be clear, I believe every comedian in this book, while on stage, was only trying to make people laugh, and they made me laugh. One of the reasons the book changed direction was I feared hanging the comedians and other interviewees out to dry by publishing their words out of context. All of them had been brave and honest in cooperating with the book, knowing the reception their actions and thoughts might provoke online. To try and temper that I switched to transcripts, including my own side of the conversation, none of which was intended to go in the book when those words were spoken. The result is that anyone who reads this book witnesses me sucking up, misunderstanding and, more importantly, failing to unpick things I would otherwise have unpicked. So I'm in the book with the best of intentions, but as one person at my publisher said, at times it makes me sound sycophantic, narcissistic and silly. I felt that was a price worth paying. Away from the world of comedy clubs, thanks to William Fiennes, who introduced me to Joseph Mitchell. It might not be obvious, but Mitchell's story 'The Old House at Home' influenced this book. Thanks to everyone at Cursor for helping me get ready for America. Thanks to my agent, Toby Mundy, especially for not objecting to appearing in the book. Thanks to everyone at my publisher, Scribe, including Adam Howard, Aoife Datta, Guy Ivison, Kevin O'Brien, Mick Pilkington, Molly Slight and Sarah Braybrooke, all of whom never complained when I was struggling to balance parenthood and deadlines. Thanks to my editor Philip Gwyn Jones. Thanks to the Society of Authors for a grant in the early days of the book. Thanks to the Arts Council for a grant in the latter days of the book. Thanks to my parents and their partners. But thanks mostly to my wife and three children, who put up with that dreadful thing of having a writer in the house. You make me laugh and I love you.

NOTES

Pages 1–4   Interview, October 26, 2018.

Pages 5–6   Interview, October 11, 2018.

Pages 7–11   Interview, October 18, 2018.

Pages 12–13   Louis on stage, October 9, 2018.

Pages 14–15   Louis on stage, October 8, 2018.

Page 16   Interview, October 26, 2018.

Pages 17–18   Interview, October 11, 2018.

Pages 19–20   Interview, September 20, 2018.

Pages 21–24   Interview, September 4, 2018.

Page 25   Ted on stage, September 1, 2019.

Page 26   Tweet from @DanaAndJulia, August 31, 2018.

Page 27   Interview, October 11, 2018.

Pages 28–30   Interview, September 4, 2018.

Pages 31–32   Louis on stage, August 27, 2018.

Pages 34–36   Interview, September 4, 2018.

Pages 37–41   Text in an email, text dated August 7, 2018.

Pages 42–44   Interview, September 20, 2018.

Page 45   Email, sent November 8, 2018.

Pages 46–48   Interview, October 26, 2018.

Pages 49–50   Email, sent June 23, 2018.

Pages 51–53   Interview, June 21, 2018.

Pages 54–55   Interview, July 18, 2018.

Pages 129–130   Erika's email, sent July 18, 2016.

Pages 135–137   Interview, July 4, 2016.

Pages 138–140   Interview, May 1, 2017.

Page 141   Interview, February 28, 2019.

Page 142   Interview, February 25, 2018.

Pages 143–145   Interview, July 11, 2017.

Pages 146–147   Interview, August 8, 2016.

Pages 148–150   Tweets, December 30, 2014.

Pages 151–153   Interview, June 27, 2017.

Pages 154–155   Interview, June 14, 2017.

Pages 156–158   Interview, July 4, 2017.

Page 159   Interview, February, 2013.

Pages 160–161   Interview, April 19, 2018.

Page 162   Interview, July 4, 2016.

Page 163   Interview, August 8, 2016.

Pages 164–167   Interview, June 3, 2017.

Pages 168–169   Interview, March 18, 2015.

Page 170   Interview, May 9, 2017.

Pages 171–172   Interview, June 16, 2017.

Page 173   Interview, September 14, 2018.

Page 174   Interview, October 26, 2018.

Page 175   Interview, July 13, 2017.

Pages 176–177   YouTube clip, uploaded July 5, 2010.

Pages 178–179   Interview, July 13, 2017.

Pages 180–182   Interview, October 18, 2018.

Pages 183–185   Interview, August 3, 2018.

Page 186   Interview, July 18, 2016.

Page 187   Interview, August 8, 2016.

Pages 188–195   Email, sent to Pat April 24, 2010.

Pages 196–199   Interview, February, 2013.

Pages 200–203   Interview, August 3, 2017.

Pages 204–205   Interview, April 19, 2018.

Pages 206–207   Electronic document, dated September 6, 2004.

Pages 208–211   Electronic document, written January, 2004.

Page 212   Interview, November 30, 2018.

Pages 213–215   Interview, February, 2013.

Page 216   Interview, October 11, 2018.

Pages 217–218   Interview, February 28, 2019.

Pages 219–220   Interview, March 18, 2015.

Page 221   Interview, July 17, 2017.

Page 222   Interview, October 8, 2018.

Pages 223–224   Interview, May 16, 2019.

Page 225   Interview, July 13, 2017.

Pages 226–228   Letter, undated.

Pages 229–230   Interview, March 18, 2015.

Page 231   Interview, August 3, 2017.

Page 232   Interview, July 14, 2017.

Page 233   Interview, June 10, 2017.

Page 234   Interview, August 6, 2017.

Page 235   Interview, July 17, 2017.

Page 236   Interview, June 6, 2017.

Pages 237–238   Interview, May 23, 2013.

Page 239   Interview, 19 April, 2018.

Pages 240–245   Petition, dated April, 2002.

Page 246   Email, sent August 7, 2016.

Page 247   Interview, July 15, 2016.

Page 248   Interview, March 18, 2015.

Pages 250–251   Interview, July 15, 2016.

Pages 252–253   Interview, March 18, 2015.

Pages 254–257   Interview, July 21, 2017.

Page 258   Interview, July 17, 2017.

Page 259   Interview, June 12, 2017.

Page 260   Interview, February 28, 2019.

Page 261   Interview, March 7, 2019.

Page 262   Interview, October 8, 2018.

Pages 263–264   Interview, June 12, 2017.

Page 265   Interview, July 31, 2017.

Pages 266–268   Interview, May 9, 2018.

Pages 269–270   Interview, October 10, 2018.

Page 271   Interview, August 13, 2018.

Pages 272–273   Interview, August 3, 2017.

Page 274   Interview, August 13, 2018.

Page 275   Interview, March 3, 2017.

Pages 276–278   Interview, March 17, 2019.

Pages 279–280   Interview, July 14, 2017.

Page 281   Email, sent August 28, 2019.

Page 282   Emails, sent August 29, 2019.

Pages 283–288   Interview, May 5, 2017.

Pages 289–290   Interview, February 28, 2019.

Pages 291–294   Larry's interviews, 1995.

Pages 295–296   Electronic letter, dated 1994 by the Office of
                  the Mayor.

Pages 297–298   Interview, May 9, 2018.

Page 299   Interview, May 5, 2017.

Page 300   Interview, May 1, 2017.

Page 301   Interview, November 28, 2018.

Pages 302–303   Interview, May 16, 2019.

Page 304   Interview, October 11, 2018.

Pages 305–306   Interview, May 16, 2019.

Page 307   Interview, September 24, 2019.

Pages 308–309   Interview, March 7, 2019.

Page 310   Interview, February, 2013.

Pages 311–312   Interview, May 31, 2017.

Page 313   Interview, June 5, 2017.

Page 314   Interview, July 18, 2018.

Page 315   Bill on stage in a video, labelled 1989.

Pages 316–317   Interview, February, 2013.

Page 318   Interview, March 7, 2019.

Pages 319–320   Interview, March 17, 2019.

Pages 321–322   Interview, March 7, 2019.

Page 323   Interview, November 8, 2018.

Pages 324–325   Interview, April 3, 2018.

Page 326   Interview, May 17, 2017.

Page 327   Interview, February 15, 2019.

Page 328   Interview, November 1, 2018.

Page 329   Interview, March 17, 2019.

Page 330   Interview, June 21, 2018.

Pages 331–332   Interview, July 13, 2017.

Page 333   Interview, July 3, 2017.

Page 334   Interview, July 3, 2017.

Pages 335–336   Interview, June 1, 2017.

Page 337   Interview, May 31, 2017

Page 340   Interview, June 14, 2017.

Pages 341–342   Interview, May 29, 2017.

Pages 343–344   Interview, July 14, 2017.

Page 345   Interview, July 15, 2016.
Page 346   Interview, March 7, 2019.
Page 347   Interview, March 18, 2015.
Pages 348–349   Interview, February 28, 2019.
Pages 350–352   Interview, February, 2013.
Page 353   Liner notes written by Manny for his band the
                  Feenjon Group's album *Jerusalem of Gold.*
Page 354   Interview, February, 2013.
Page 355   Liner notes written by Manny for the Feenjon
                  Group's album *Songs of Israel and Other Places,*
                  copyrighted 1977.
Pages 356–357   Interview, February 28, 2019.
Pages 358–360   Interview, July 12, 2017.
Pages 364–369   Interview, October 9, 2019.